RAVE REVIEWS FOR
FROM DOPE TO HOPE: A MAN IN RECOVERY

"I, like Tim Ryan, hate the opiate epidemic that has gripped our nation. How did we get here? The fundamental answer is one tragic story, one grieving family at a time. This is the addict's journey: how it happens, how it progresses, and how it ends. Fortunately, this is also the journey of recovery: how it happens and how it blossoms. There is always hope."

—"Dr. Drew" Pinsky, M.D.

"This book and its author offer an important contribution to an issue that impacts all of our communities. Now more than ever, we know that opioid and heroin abuse is a treatable medical condition and not a moral failing. I hope we will be able to end this addiction's public stigma and find treatments for those who suffer from it."

—Congressman Bill Foster

"Tim Ryan has lived an extraordinary life, depending on one's perception. Tim was a very successful entrepreneur at the age of 22, accompanied with an office in the Wrigley Building (downtown Chicago). Little did he know, his addiction would soon consume everything in his life, including his son, Nick, who would overdose. It was through that horrible day that Tim was reborn. Today, Tim has 4 1/2 years sober and spends every waking moment helping one addict at a time to overcome addiction. How many people can say they have lived two lives in one lifetime? Tim can."

—Brandon Novak, Actor

"Passion is what fuels Tim Ryan to do what he does every day. Tim's personal story highlights the growing heroin and opioid epidemic that is afflicting every gender, age, and socio-economic background across northern Illinois and the country. Heroin is tearing our communities and families apart, and it's time for a wake-up call. Tim's story from the front lines of the opioid epidemic forces us to learn and encourages us to act."

—Congressman Randy Hultgren (IL-14)

"To say that my friend, Tim, has 'walked the walk' would too simply understate the way in which he's brought his passion for recovery advocacy to the battlefield of the addiction epidemic. As you turn these pages, you will discover a man who plummeted to one of the most painful and desperate plateaus in what is commonly referred to as 'the bottom' in the recovery community. The desperation of his addiction, the consequences he suffered, and the dark moment of his greatest loss culminated into the kind of devastation that most of us couldn't survive. But Tim survived—and so much more. He dove headlong into the miraculous journey of recovery and new life that usually involves a lifetime of self-preservation that is necessary for most addicts and alcoholics. Instead, though, Tim found a new fuel for his boundless engine of energy and has thrown himself into a relentlessly dedicated battle to save as many lives as possible from the disease that stole so much from him.

...The 12th Step reads as follows: 'Having had a spiritual awakening as the result of these steps, we tried to carry this message to alcoholics, and to practice these principles in all our affairs.' For most of us in the recovery community, this means setting up and breaking down chairs after meetings, 'sponsoring' another fellow addict, and speaking at meetings or in the community when we can. I don't mean to discount any of these actions, as they are important, exhausting, and crucial to the journey of recovery. But for Tim Ryan, the 12th Step has become an entire way of life. He is 'on call' 24 hours a day, seven days a week, 365 days a year. There are no holidays, no reprieves, and no escapes from his commitment to the cause.

... As you get to know Tim through this book, you will undoubtedly marvel at the catastrophic pain of his addiction. I believe, though, that you will much more fully marvel at the new life that this man has chosen to live and the dedication he's shown to the well-being of others suffering from this unforgiving disease. I hope that you will find as much inspiration in these pages as I've found in knowing Tim. And I hope that you will carry this inspiration into your life—and in your own devotion to your battles and advocacy for the battles of others."

—**David Dastmalchian, Actor**

FROM DOPE TO HOPE:
A MAN IN RECOVERY

BY
TIM RYAN

FROM DOPE TO HOPE: A MAN IN RECOVERY

ISBN: 978-0-9845917-2-5

Cover Design by: Phil Davis

Interior Design by: Amanda Heinrich, AGraphicStyle.com

Published by: Spiritus Communications, SpiritusCommunications.com, (919)732-5549

DEDICATION

This book is dedicated to my son,

Nicholas James Hoban Ryan.

I am sorry I was not a father to you. I was a friend.

If I could turn back time, trust me, I would.

You are always with me, my son.

You are the driving force for me each and every day.

—Dad

TABLE OF CONTENTS

FOREWORD

As the executive clinical director at Banyan Treatment Center Chicago, I have 20 years of experience in the mental health field. I've seen a lot of things and met a lot of people, but I have never met anyone quite like Tim Ryan.

When I first met Tim, he was outspoken, driven, and very rough around the edges. My pastor had called me one day, three years ago, and asked if I had any interest in leading a support group for families of those affected by substance use disorders. The group was an excellent way to help the community during an epidemic; but then I learned that it came with Tim as a partner. I questioned myself working with a felon who was still on parole, with no professional background or credentials. I had worked for decades on my career and credentials. *What could someone like Tim possibly offer?*

Despite my reservations, I stepped out in boldness and faith. I said yes to the support group, and I said yes to Tim Ryan. I am passionate about working with people affected by substance use disorders; the support group provided the forum for a much-needed open dialogue in our community.

I saw people come in feeling ashamed, lost, angry, hurt, and fearful of their loved ones dying from this disease that no one speaks of. Tim was able to demystify their struggles in a manner that was different from that of most professionals.

There was not much that Tim wouldn't share. He shared his pain—from years of using drugs and drowning in guilt, shame, trauma, compulsion, and lies. I saw him literally sit on the ground with people who wanted an escape from the cycle of insanity. He shared his hope: what it took for him to surrender and work the process of recovery. I witnessed him hold the hands of countless individuals and families and lead them to professional help.

I quickly realized that Tim brought something raw, true, and heartfelt that transcended professional techniques and interventions. What he offered was his humanness and an unrelenting pursuit to give to others what he had been missing for so many years—a path to recovery and hope.

But Tim's journey was not complete; neither was his heartache. Over the next year, I thought Tim's own subsequent tragic losses would be the tipping point for our work with the support group—if not the tipping point for Tim in his recovery. His grief process was, and still is, deeply painful. He carries the heavy burden of his personal losses daily. I watched Tim carefully during these times, but he only dug deeper and had more resolve than ever to help others battle this disease.

The support group continued weekly at the church, and we quickly ran out of chairs. Sadly, many nights we saw standing room only, as the epidemic of addiction took more lives in our community. Tim and I volunteered more hours of work for the community. It was just *the right thing to do.*

For two years, we worked together. I was the consummate professional, stubbornly holding to ethical and industry standards. Tim was the transformative *man in recovery*, proposing ever bigger ideas with little concern for practical matters. During one meeting, he turned to me and said, "Maybe we should open a treatment center."

I laughed and said, "NO WAY."

Tim had street credentials and passion; but he had so much to learn about mental health and substance use disorder treatment. We had many arguments, usually involving a lot of cursing, before finding common ground in our mutual desire to restore health and hope to those who were suffering.

Tim quickly learned about the mental health industry— enough to land an outreach position with Banyan Treatment Center in Florida. I maintained my work in private practice, as

Tim continued to press the issue of opening a treatment center in Illinois. I repeatedly turned him down, but he wouldn't give up.

Eventually, he convinced me to go to Florida to meet the Banyan owner and staff. After touring the facility, I agreed to help Banyan obtain a license to provide treatment in Illinois. I also agreed to assume the position of clinical director and close my private practice. It seemed that Tim Ryan was rubbing off on me.

In order for Tim to work directly with Banyan Treatment Center Chicago, we had to request an exemption wherein his work was under my direction and professional licensure for a two-year period. If you had asked me when I met Tim if I could foresee myself risking my license to allow him to work in a treatment setting, I would have said *absolutely not*. And I would have been wrong in that assumption.

Over the span of two years, Tim earned my respect, my admiration, and most importantly, my trust. I watched him transform into a person for whom I was willing to put myself on the line. For the lives that he would help, and for the person I had come to know, he was worth the risk.

On November 18th, 2015, I was given the keys to Banyan Treatment Center Chicago. As Tim and I walked into the open space, I turned to him and said, "Maybe we should open a treatment center." We laughed, we cried, and we prayed for all that would enter to find what Tim Ryan has found: a life in recovery.

—Suzette Papadakis MS, LCPC, NCC,
CGT Executive Clinical Director,
Banyan Treatment Center Chicago

ACKNOWLEDGMENTS

I would like to thank some people who helped guide me down this road to recovery.

Shannon Ryan, you are the one person who always stuck by my side—along with Tom and Pat Ryan, my parents.

To my children—Nick, Max, Tanner, Abby, and little Mackenzie—I owe you my world.

Kirstin, thanks for being my jib.

To John, my sponsor; Steve M.; and Suzette Papadakis, my friend, mentor, and business partner—thank you for supporting me every day on this road called recovery. Rich Wistocki, you are "the cop" who went to bat for me and became a dear friend, and I owe you deep gratitude. Eric K., Tracen G., Randy D., and so many more—we are all in this together, and I thank you.

Joe Tuttle, you are the man who gave me a career and a life I could not have today without you.

Denise Crosby, thank you for the many articles on the opiate epidemic, which are taking this issue out of the shadows and offering help.

Thank you to Bill Leff and Wendy Snyder of WGN Radio for all you do to support A Man in Recovery Foundation.

Scott and Jocelyn Carbonara of Spiritus Communications, thank you for writing my book.

To the chief of police in Dixon, Illinois, Danny Langloss, Jr.; Brian Cunningham, the chief of police in Woodridge, Illinois; the Naperville police department; the city of Naperville's mayor, Steve Chirico, and the city council—thank you for your never-tiring support, expertise, and focus on curbing this epidemic.

Thank you to Congressman Bill Foster and Congressman Randy Hultgren for listening and helping. Thank you to Rob and Susan Russell. Thank you to Matt Ganem, the friend who started me on my mission, and Brandon Novak, for all your work today. Darek Horan, Brad Gerkhe, and Kyle Simari—thank you for putting up with my shit.

To all my brothers and sisters in recovery and of course my GOD—thank you, from the bottom of my heart!

INTRODUCTION

My name is Tim Ryan, and I'm an alcoholic and drug addict. I know addiction better than most, because I lived it for 30 years. You name it, I've done it—booze, LSD, angel dust, cocaine, crystal meth, amphetamines, and heroin.

I became addicted to many of them. But heroin quickly became my drug of choice.

Heroin is the drug that killed my fearless and carefree son and tried to kill me, too.

This book details my battles against the addictions that nearly took everything. Heroin caused me to overdose eight times and be pronounced clinically dead three. I've had two minor heart attacks. I've been arrested more than 10 times. I shouldn't be here.

Heroin didn't make me a better person. It stole more than half of my life. In fact, I can't think of a single good thing that came as a result of my heroin use. But I can give you a long list of things and people I've lost because of it.

And yet I'm still alive.

The difference is that today I know *why* I'm still alive: I'm a man on a mission. I'm an alcoholic and drug addict, but today I live to make a positive difference in this world. My entire life revolves around helping others find hope and recovery.

I call my story *"a man in recovery."* I'm just one man. Others have danced with the devil and lived to tell about it. Some found paths to recovery that are different from mine. There is no wrong way to get there. *"Thank God you got clean,"* is what I say to anyone who finds himself on the other side of an addiction like mine.

But this is my story. Besides telling you *how I did it* and *how I do it* every day, I'll offer you my opinions and insights. I'll do my best to faithfully tell my story. I'll tell you how I found recovery, how I stay in recovery, and—if you're an addict, this applies to you—how *you can receive the gift of recovery yourself.*

Where there is life, there is hope. As long as you have breath, you have hope. If this book is in your hands right now, you have hope. And if you are reading this because a loved one has been caught in the pit of addiction, you need to know that there is hope.

I'm not exaggerating when I say that I'm an expert on addiction. I don't rely on my Ph.D. or M.D. degrees (I have neither). My expertise comes from real-world experience in the field—the years I spent chasing down heroin until eventually it took over my life. I'm an expert in recovery, because of my prison time offering me a clear, simple choice: recover or die.

Read this book, and you'll better understand when I say that my parents, siblings, friends, and community didn't make me an addict. I made choices that took me down the road to addiction. But very quickly, the drugs began making choices for me.

You will learn how I made and lost millions. You will meet the women I manipulated throughout my life so I could use them, just as my addictions were using me. You will come with me as I lie, cheat, and steal my way across the country to feed my growing demons. You will rot with me in a state prison cell I shared with gang leaders you've read about in the news. You will break down with me as I come face to face with repentance and finally acknowledge how many lives I harmed. You will rejoice with me when I find recovery. And finally, I hope you will join me on this crusade to help others who struggle between life and death— battling heroin or other drugs.

Do you think I'm overstating the devastation of an addiction—and particularly to heroin? I mean, we all know people who abuse drugs for years, and they're still kicking.

If you smoke cigarettes, you can expect a shortened life expectancy, and you'll likely die of emphysema, lung cancer, or heart disease. An addiction to tobacco will kill you.

If you're an alcoholic, you might wreck your car, maybe killing yourself or innocent people in the process. Or maybe you'll lose it all, live on the streets, and die from exposure or cirrhosis of the liver. An addiction to alcohol will kill you.

Living as a heroin addict, and now living to help addicts find recovery, however, I've learned the difference between alcohol and heroin. If you lock a hundred people in a room for a week and ply them with large amounts of alcohol, you should expect anywhere from 10 to 20 percent of them to go on to become full-blown alcoholics. That's serious and nothing to joke about.

But if you lock a hundred people in a room for a week and ply them with large amounts of heroin (and you can add legally or illegally obtained pain medication, opiates, and benzos like Xanax, Klonopin, and Valium), when you open those doors, you should expect that 100 percent of them will be full-blown drug addicts.

How addictive are heroin and other opiates? Once you are addicted, you will find recovery, end up in prison, or die. The draw is that strong. You will steal to support your habit. You will willingly risk every friend, every loved one, and everything that you once cherished just to get high again. And you'll do it even if it kills you. And too often, it does. Over the last two years, I have attended 100-plus funerals of those who lost their battles to addiction. And every day this number grows, as the wreckage of this unforgiving disease progresses and destroys more lives and families.

How deadly is heroin? Yesterday morning, I spoke to a great young man. I met him after he overdosed on heroin. I begged him to enter recovery. I told him that he was lucky to be alive, and I assured him that if he would give recovery a try, I would be there for him every step of the way. He told me that he would think about it.

He was dead before the sun went down.

I hate this drug. I hate how it kills our children, our brothers and sisters, our neighbors, our friends, and our communities. I fucking hate this drug and the carnage it leaves in its wake.

It breaks my heart when addicts say, "*I'm not stupid. That won't happen to me.*" Until it does. The drug makes them believe they are invincible. The drug lies to them, and they eagerly accept each lie, because it is what they want to believe. Some will overdose, go the brink of death like I did, and come back with an arrogant laugh of "*See? I told you! Nothing can kill me!*" Until it does.

I wrote this book to out my shame, as a way of deepening my ongoing commitment to recovery. All addicts bury a lot of deep pain beneath the guilt and blurry memories. That misery will either kill you or drive you to recovery. I wrote this book to tell the truth—even the truth that most people wish they could ignore. This story is the unraveling of my painful story. You may see yourself in my story. You may see none of yourself. My prayer is that either way, you will find hope.

Recovery is healing me, but it's never over. It's something I choose to do every day. I choose recovery like it's a matter of life or death, because it is. I've wept over dozens of friends who left recovery to have "one last hurrah" before getting serious about it. All it took is one relapse, and the drug claimed their lives. I fucking hate this drug.

My past provided a training ground to my battlefield today. Five years ago, I spent every waking moment with one obsessive thought: *how do I score the next fix?* My battle is no longer about finding the next high. It's about bringing people to the recovery God gave me to offer. My training ground allowed me to walk into a house with a desperate family and walk out with an addict ranging in age from 12 to 78 a couple of hours later to get him into treatment. The individual usually feels so trapped that he's given up. He's burned through every resource. And now he's just waiting to die. I offer him help. And that help starts with offering him *hope.*

I have a lot of regrets, but I have to focus on the beauty of my life today. It's still chaotic like anyone's—trying to balance everything I do to the best of my abilities—but every day I put my recovery first. I can't be of service to anyone without it.

Some have called me "the addict whisperer," "a miracle worker," or "the general," because of my zeal in heading the charge to lead others to recovery. It doesn't go to my head. I'm grateful to God every moment I live because of the greatest gift He's given me: recovery. I am able to work with the hopeless, because I was once hopeless.

Today, because of that gift of recovery, I run A Man in Recovery Foundation; speak in schools, prisons, and courthouses, and anywhere else that they'll have me; and place people who suffer from addictions in facilities all over the country.

As a heroin addict, *I shouldn't be here.* Too many of my dear friends and family members are *no longer here* because of this awful drug. But as a man in recovery, God has other plans for me. Each day I commit to making living amends to those I hurt, those I failed, and those I helped lead into addiction. God has me in the thick of it, because He wants me to make a difference in the lives of others.

My hope is that if you are in the throes of addiction, you will hear that still, small voice telling you, *"Your story doesn't have to end here."* My prayer is that after reading my story, you will trust me when I say that recovery doesn't suck. In fact, my life is fuller now than it's ever been. And I know that with God's help, it will get better still. And yours can, too.

My name is Tim Ryan, and I'm an alcoholic and a drug addict. But by the grace of God, my Higher Power, I found recovery. And that's the only reason I'm here today. From dope to hope, and with the continued grace of God, I will remain a man in recovery.

CHAPTER 1

AFTER THE CRASH

"Tim Ryan, please rise," the bailiff called. My stomach tightened. My legs didn't want to support my weight as I slowly stood upright. This was the moment I had been dreading. The heroin in my system made me numb, but not numb enough to block out what was about to happen.

"Fuck!" I muttered in disbelief as I found myself stuck between freedom and imprisonment. "Fuck."

As always, I'd gone to court alone that day—just me and my lawyer. There was no sense in dragging anyone else with me. After all, I'd gotten there by my own doing.

My wife, Shannon, had driven me to the train station near our home in Oswego, a western suburb of Chicago. That train would take me into Chicago, where I would stand before the judge in a few hours' time. My then 12-year-old daughter, Abby, sat quietly in the back seat. The three of us found little to talk about on the drive. It was raining, which seemed fitting. No one wanted to go anywhere on a day like that. My mood was especially dark, because I was going somewhere I didn't want to go. I knew that I'd be gone for a long time. To make matters worse, I had absolutely no control over the situation.

I finally broke the silence of the drive. "Shannon, they're taking me today. I won't be coming back."

"You say that every time you go to court," she said. "I'll see you tonight."

Denial soothed her for the moment. I didn't share her outlook. I knew better.

"I'm serious," I said. "If you try to call me after 10 o'clock and my phone is off, they took me."

"Yeah," she said shaking her head, believing all would be fine. "I'll see you tonight."

I jumped out of the car, kissed my wife and daughter, and hopped on the train that would take me to my fate.

The courthouse would not be my first or last stop of the day. I had some "business" to take care of before I got there. I knew after court, I would be taken to a holding cell. And after that, prison. I'd seen all the movies. I knew people who had been to the "big house."

Who am I kidding? I'd already been a *guest* of the state prison system once before, so I knew full well what to expect. As scared as I was of what could happen to me inside those prison walls, I was even more scared of what was about to take place inside of my own body.

In the days and weeks ahead of this appointed hour, I didn't back off my heroin use. Hell, I doubled-down. I knew that once the drugs started to leave my system, I would be dope sick. Then I was going to detox hard. It could kill me, and there would be times in the process that I would wish that it would; I knew that much.

So I did what addicts do: I scored more drugs. First thing on the morning of my court sentencing, I called my drug dealer. Once I got off the train in the city, I took a cab and met him right by his house, which is not something drug dealers usually let you do. I guess I got lucky that day. More likely, my dealer wasn't willing to pass up making some "easy money" on such a good, loyal customer. I had a $500 a day habit. I wasn't stupid enough to think my dealer loved me; but I knew he loved my money.

I bought 60 bags of heroin. I snorted 10 bags on the five-minute cab ride to the courthouse. I stashed the rest in a hole I made in my jacket. I wanted to take enough smack with me so I wouldn't be feverishly dope sick in the holding cell.

And I desperately hoped that once I got into Cook County Jail, I could see the doctor to help me detox properly.

I'd been to prison once before, in 2008. I told myself that I would never go back. If you're wondering what sent me there the first time, it was something stupid: driving on four revokes. That sounds innocent enough. Drugs had no part in my arrest; it was due to my driving with a revoked license. But where do you think I was going without a license every time I got pulled over? To buy heroin. And why do you think my license got revoked in the first place? For my DUIs. Yeah, drugs and alcohol had been driving me for years.

The cop who pulled me over the second time I was caught driving with a revoked license was "Officer Fred" of the Chicago Police Department. He was a nice guy. I thought it then, and I still think it now. He was just doing his job to keep the streets safe from people like me who get doped up and then kill people with their vehicles. He told me to stop driving and cited me.

"Yeah, officer, I'm so sorry." I tried to sound as repentant as I could, and for those few minutes, I probably was. I found another ride home that night.

Eight months later, I got pulled over for the fourth time with a revoked license. Yeah, nothing changed.

Do you know what else didn't change? Who do you think pulled me over that time? Officer Fred from the Chicago Police Department. I was driving a different vehicle. That was the only change from eight months earlier.

I either had the worst luck in the world, or God had a plan for me that He was working even before I acknowledged His existence.

The officer approached my car and motioned me to roll down my window. "Man, you look familiar," he said.

"Officer Fred, good to see you. You stopped me eight months ago," I said, wondering in the back of my head if there was even the slightest possibility that my charming personality would get me out of this mess.

"Damn it, I told you to quit driving," he said, shaking his head. He took my identification and returned to his squad car.

He was gone for so long, I started to believe that he might let me go with a little verbal lashing.

"Tim, this is a felony, man. I gotta take you in." He cuffed me.

As a result of that arrest, I spent a year in prison. Back then, a year meant that you got out after 61 days if you were a good boy. I made sure that I was good for 61 days. I counted off each day, making little lines like a prisoner in an old movie, scratching tick marks on the cell walls. I served my time quietly and went right back out there.

I may have paid my debt to society, but I was still an addict with a diseased mind when I got out. While I told myself on my first visit to the joint in 2008 that I would never go back, nothing changed in my drug use. *Nothing changed.*

As I sat on the train speeding towards the city that morning of my sentencing, I knew that today I wasn't going to get a slap on the wrist. I had hired the best lawyer money could buy, and he was able to delay my case for 21 months. But this time, matters were more serious. Way more serious.

Once I got inside the courthouse, I had to surrender my coat and other personal items. *Please don't find my stash,* I thought as I handed over my belongings. Then I settled into the seat next to my lawyer and waited.

Despite the heroin coursing through my body, my legs shook nervously under the table.

I thought of my wife, kids, and parents, and I wished to God that I could blame them for some part—any part—of this situation. But this had nothing to do with them. This was about my problem, not theirs. They were as perfect as a family could be, and somehow I fucked it all up. And now I was going to pay for it. Even though they had no fault in this, they would have to pay for it, too.

"Tim Ryan, please rise," the bailiff called out, shaking me out of my head.

I told myself that once I got out of this current mess, there was no way in hell that I would ever go back to prison. I was wrong. I would go back inside. But the circumstances surrounding my return to prison would be very different.

Presiding over my case was Judge Willis, a distinguished, gray-haired gentleman. My lawyer told me he was a Sox fan and a fair man. I didn't want fair; I wanted forgiving. I wanted a push-over.

My lawyer approached the bench, and I heard Judge Willis muttering something like, "10-12, 10-12."

I gathered from those words that Judge Willis wanted to give me 12 years. I looked at my lawyer with a shrug in need of an answer. He mouthed, "Hold on, hold on."

My lawyer and the judge continued talking, and then I heard the judge say, "3-3-1."

My lawyer walked back from the bench and stood next to me. I searched his face for some sort of answer, but at that same moment the judge announced his sentence: "Seven years."

The gavel dropped along with my hopes of a cake-walk sentence.

"What?" I asked my lawyer. "What is 3-3-1? Am I going away for seven years?"

"No, listen. You got seven years total for all charges. You got three years, three years, and one year. With good behavior, you'll be out in a year and a half."

Whew. I had done two months before. Eighteen months was a helluva lot better than the 7, 10, or 12 years that I could have gotten.

Immediately, the bailiff took me into the back, and my thoughts shifted to *how can I get my heroin into the cell with me right the fuck now?*

CHAPTER 2

MY START

When people know a little bit about my heroin addiction and prison time, they immediately assume that I had a shitty childhood. I can see some people size me up, and I can just about read their minds: *"So you must have come from a home full of abuse, neglect, abandonment, maybe incest, the works—right?"*

But I didn't. My childhood was wonderful. My parents were the greatest, most loving parents in the world, and they are still my best friends to this day. My dad worked at E.F. Hutton for 26 years and never called in sick, not even once. He was a humble man and role model, and he was incredibly loyal to the family. He loved my mom more than anything in the world, and he still does.

My parents couldn't have children of their own. But they had so much love to share, they adopted me; my older brother, Sam, who is two years older than me; and Carrie and Cameron, my younger siblings.

Sam and I fought all the time. Most of it was just typical kid shit. Once Sam spent six months building a huge battleship. I destroyed it the next day, knowing that he was going to kick my ass for it. But I did it anyway. We were that kind of brothers.

My relationship with Carrie and Cameron was very different. They are three-quarters Chippewa Indian twins, and they got the worst kind of racial slurs thrown at them. More than once, I started fist-fights standing up for them. In my relationship with Sam, I felt like I needed protecting from him. He enjoyed beating me up day after day. But with Cameron and Carrie, I learned to look out for and protect those two.

My family always ate dinner together at 6:30 sharp every night. Mom would ring the bell outside our house, and we'd come running. Unlike other families who ate off trays in front of the TV or sat together only on holidays, we usually gathered around the kitchen table and talked with each other while dining. We discussed what went on in our lives.

When I was very little, my family didn't have much money. We ate shit-on-a-shingle a lot. You could feed a lot of people from a cheap, slow-cooked roast with gravy poured over toast. As a kid, I never felt deprived. We ate well, and I never considered the challenge my parents must have faced going from feeding themselves—to feeding themselves and four growing kids.

On the weekend, we'd work together. I felt good contributing to the household, and I cherished those times. We would clean house, cut grass, rake leaves, wash the car, and do the things that families without money often do to pitch in.

My dad's father had built the first houses on the lake in Crystal Lake, Illinois—a town about 30 miles northwest of where we lived in Mount Prospect, Illinois. My grandfather was born in 1880, and for one reason or another, he flip-flopped between being a pauper and a millionaire. At 63, he married my grandmother, who was 40.

When I was four, my dad knocked on the door of one of the houses my grandfather had built and owned years earlier, before he lost it to the bank. A man answered.

"My father built this house, so it's very special to me," Dad told the guy in the doorway. "So, if you ever want to sell, I'd like to buy it."

Timing is everything. The owner was ready to move on, and my dad purchased that house on the lake. For my dad, it was like coming home.

Dad's mom, my grandmother, "Floey," lived directly behind us. Floey's age went with the years. In 1978, she was 78; in 1979, she was 79; and so on. Every day as a little kid I'd go over there, and she'd make me eggs and bacon. My absolute favorite was when she'd make "swirls," which were small, delicious cinnamon rolls with icing dripping off the top. My brother, Sam, once crammed three into his mouth at one time. So I immediately stuffed four into my own trap.

The way my family lived was no different than most of the people I knew. We had a great life. We always knew we were loved.

I got the belt twice. There were no beatings in my home. As my dad's job started to pay more, my parents spent more money updating the house. We were the first ones on the block with an electric garage door opener. Shortly after we got it, my brother and I took turns pushing the button up and down for hours. Once the novelty of that wore off, we invited the neighborhood kids to hang on the door while we repeatedly pushed the magic button. Our play didn't last long, because we broke the damn thing. The small motor charged with lifting the door—on wheels and tracks—didn't hold up to the weight of the door and six boys.

When my dad came home from work and discovered our crime, he said, "You are going to get one swat for every hour it takes me to fix this." And then he said something that I knew to be true: "It's going to hurt me more than it hurts you." It took him two hours to fix it. Those weren't easy hours. We'd done a real number on it. When Dad was done, true to his word, he disciplined us. My brother and I got two whacks on our asses.

The second licking came when my brother and I knocked down my grandmother's Christmas tree while horsing around.

Obviously, we deserved a lot more lickings than we got. But my parents were pretty calm and low-key. It took a lot to upset them. Which is a good thing, because if I'd had every swat I deserved, I still wouldn't be able to sit down.

I wasn't a bad kid, but I was curious and adventurous. I was always fishing and playing on that lake, whether it was canoeing or ice skating. I lived outside. Sam was more into playing with models and watching Saturday TV shows. He did his own thing; I did mine. Carrie and Cameron played soccer. When any one of us kids played a sport, my parents showed up, cheering and supporting us.

I loved it when my parents joined my adventures, like the time they helped me build a tree fort. I simply liked being with them. I had a great family.

People who knew me then said that I was the nicest, happiest kid. Hell, I was happy. And I had every reason to be. I lived on a lake, and the whole world existed in my own backyard. Who wouldn't be happy?

Several times when I was a little boy, my dad took me on the train to Chicago to his job at the Board of Trade. On one of those rides, my dad told me that he used to sit in the smoking and gambling car on the train. At the time, he made only $600 a month on draw. He told me that he had played poker for spending money. Once he started making real money, he quit gambling. And once he started making money, he gave us kids everything we needed and most of the things we could ever want.

"Growing up, my family went on only two vacations," my dad told our family.

"Why?" I asked him. "Didn't you like going on vacation?"

"Of course we liked it," he said, shaking his head. "But we didn't have the money. We could either eat three meals a day, or we could take a trip. We couldn't afford to do both. So we ate."

My dad wanted more for us—and better. As he started making more money, we'd go see my grandparents—who had moved down to Sarasota, Florida—every Christmas or spring break. Then we started the tradition of a canoe trip on the Wisconsin River. We'd go to Shotgun Eddie's and do some whitewater rafting while there. We'd rent an RV and go somewhere else another time of year. Once we went snow skiing in Colorado.

Another thing you should know about my parents is that they weren't big drinkers. The only time I saw my dad get a little loopy is when he took us fishing in Canada way up into the boundary waters. His buddy, Tommy, brought 70 cases of beer in his boat. Tommy owned a bar, so this man had experience with offering drinks to those around him. Whenever he'd offer a beer, my dad would take it graciously. I think Dad lost track of how many beers he was polishing off, and he got a little tipsy on that trip. But even that time Dad was over-served, he kept a protective eye on us kids to make sure we were safe.

My parents always seemed to do the right thing, the smart thing. When they learned that smoking caused cancer, they quit, simple as that.

So how does someone who had a great life turn into an addict who overdoses, goes to prison, and nearly dies multiple times?

CHAPTER 3

SKIMMING THE SURFACE

For all of the things going right in my world, school was never one of them. I was a dummy. Or at least, that's how I saw myself, and I'm pretty sure that's how others saw me, too. School just wasn't for me. English, math, I didn't comprehend any of it. Verb, pronoun, I didn't know what the hell they were. I couldn't wrap my head around those concepts.

They didn't know what was wrong with me back then, but I suffered from A.D.D. and some dyslexia. My parents supported me the best way they could. From sixth grade on, they got me tutors, but I just wasn't into school.

If you fail enough times, you want to give up. Repeated failure took its toll on my self-esteem. I felt like everyone around me knew things that I couldn't begin to understand. I know now that my struggles were not related to having a low IQ. I just couldn't learn the way others did. I learned by doing, being active, and trying things my way.

I got through high school by the skin of my teeth. I got an 11 on my A.C.T. The kick in the ass is that I took it four times. My G.P.A. was a 1.4. I think the school just wanted me out. I had put in my time, and the school administration probably figured that I'd come to the end of my ability to learn. So they let me graduate.

But my learning disabilities and low esteem went with me when I entered one of only two colleges that would take me. Sitting in orientation, hearing about all the different majors I could study, I decided that I was going to be a pilot. I grew up watching *Top Gun*, so I thought, *Hell, I already have the cocky attitude. Give me a pilot's license, and I'm Tom Cruise.*

The first year in, they changed the law so you couldn't wear corrective lenses and be a pilot. I wore glasses, so that was out the window.

Great. I'm stupid as well as too blind to fly a plane. What am I going to do now? I thought to myself.

Some friends of mine majored in political science. "Yeah," I told myself. "I can do that. I can be a politician or a lawyer. They don't have to be smart. All they do is bullshit. How hard can it be?"

For me, it was hard. I took English 101 in college three times. And I failed three times. I got a 49 percent the last time, and you had to get a 51 percent to pass. I was devastated. The worst part was that I really tried.

But I did have one more dream to pursue. While I knew I would never be a rocket scientist (or a pilot, or a lawyer, or a politician, or an English teacher...), I mastered one thing better than nearly anyone else: water skiing.

When I was 10, I met a guy who would become my best friend: Randy. He lived down the lake, and he was four years older than me. I rode my bike to where he put a boat in the water and watched him ski for hours. One day, he asked me to join him and his brother.

"Hell, yeah!" I shouted.

I was a natural. I got up my first time. In no time, I got up on one ski, and shortly after that, I kicked the skis off and learned to barefoot water ski. I had a knack for it.

Water skiing takes two things: balance and guts. You need balance, because the boat jerks one way, and the waves are coming at you from all sides—small ones and big swells in the wake of the boat. You have to shift your weight constantly to keep from falling. Water skiing reminds me of when Luke Skywalker finally learned to close his eyes and trust "the force" to guide him. If you stop to think about what you're doing when a boat is pulling you at 50 miles an hour, you're going down. Hard. And it will break you in half when you hit the water. While God might not have given me a brain built for the classroom, he double-gifted me with the balance to ski.

And water skiing takes guts. What kind of idiot would hold onto a rope being pulled by a boat going 50 miles an hour? Me. If school had taught me one thing, it was that I must be an idiot. To soothe my esteem about my repeated failures in the classroom, I prided myself that I had more guts than a herd of cattle. You know what an adrenaline junkie looks like? Me. I pushed myself with a fearless drive for excellence. Taking risks fueled me. Within weeks of first getting up on skis, I was already doing things that had taken Randy—and Johnny, the top water skier in Crystal Lake—years to try.

Whenever they were out on a boat, I was with them. I logged some serious hours on the water in the sun, which is probably why I have recurring skin cancer today. What 10-year-old boy is going to put on sunscreen every hour? Besides, no one talked much about the dangers of the sun back then. Hell, people would smear baby oil all over themselves to deepen their tans.

Life was good. Randy and I would spend all summer long on his dad's 1968 Ski Nautique. We were on the lake by day, and every night Randy and I worked in a bar/pizzeria serving up pizza pies. The real fun happened on the weekends when we entered local tournaments. We loved to impress the crowds with our slalom skills and trick jumps.

In 1985 when I was 16 years old, I went to a water skiing tournament, and there I saw and fell madly in love for the first time. She was a six-month-old 1985 MasterCraft with a "for sale" on her. I ripped off the sign and gave it to my dad, along with my most winning look. He rolled his eyes.

That Fourth of July weekend, I sat on the pier with my friends, Randy and Jesse, and my mom. This red MasterCraft flew past us on the lake.

I looked at my mom, "Mom, we should get a boat like that."

We watched as that boat circled the lake twice. Then it pulled up to our pier. My dad sat behind the wheel, and my little brother, Cameron, beamed next to him along with another guy I didn't know. My jaw dropped as my dad pulled up next to us. He threw the keys to me.

"Here you go, kiddo. Now go win some tournaments."

I was so excited that I dropped the keys twice, nearly plopping them into the water.

"She's all gassed up for you," my dad said, as he slapped me on the shoulder. "But that's the last time I'll ever put gas in it. Take good care of her. She's all yours."

I was overwhelmed. I watched as my dad wrote the stranger a check for $13,000, which was a lot of money back then. Hell, it's a lot of money today! I got tears in my eyes as it hit me that he had just spent $13,000 to buy me my own ski boat. That's one of the many ways Dad showed me his love.

I loved him back. And I loved my new boat, too. We ultimately logged 4,000 hours on that motor, and I practically lived on the boat all summer long.

I became the top water skier at Crystal Lake. I could do slalom, trick, barefoot, forwards, backwards, you name it. Nobody could barefoot water ski or trick ski like me. Some might have been a little better at slalom, but I did everything. I had guts, remember? When I started competing in barefoot water skiing, I conditioned myself to get back up when I fell. And I refused to let go of the rope when I fell, because your run didn't end until you let go. That means I took some hellacious falls. Today, I have several ruptured disks in my lower back to show for it.

During this period of my life, I also started to fall in love with something else: alcohol. Back then, it didn't seem like a big deal to go out and drink the night away with great friends.

Tommy, that friend of my dad's who fished with us in Canada, owned a bar called the Pinemoor. It was huge bar and pizzeria with an upstairs converted into an old flop hotel. My brother and I started working there on weekends. I was 10 at the time. My job was to hump off hundreds of cases of beer and buckets of ice for the co-owner, Sal, who was too old to go up and down the stairs. I think we got paid $2 in cash for the morning's work, but it came with other benefits: a pack of Doublemint gum, a Hershey bar, and all the soda pop we could drink.

Being surrounded by beer, it wasn't long until I "upgraded" my soda pop to something with a little more kick. I liked the taste, but I didn't really think much of it.

At first.

When I was a freshman in high school, Randy was a senior. We were both blond haired, blue eyed, 6 feet 1 inch. We looked like twins. His birthday was 09/18/65; mine was 09/19/68. We were four years and one day apart. Randy took a road trip to visit his older brother, Doug, who was in school at Western Illinois University. Randy left Doug's place with a case of beer and then picked me up in his dad's Volaré. We drove around and drained that case of beer in a couple of hours. I came home and puked my brains out that night. That was the first time I got drunk.

It wouldn't be my last.

My dad came into the bathroom and immediately knew what was going on. "You and that damned Randy!" my dad shouted. "His dad is a police sergeant. I'm going to give him a piece of my mind. You're not hanging out with that rotten kid again!"

A week later, my dad wasn't mad. I returned to spending nights at Randy's house with the blessing of my parents, who assumed that I'd learned my lesson for having spent that one, long night with my face hanging inside the porcelain throne.

I hadn't. Nothing changed.

I mean, I wasn't drinking every day. That would have been crazy. I wasn't doing great at school, but I still had to go. But every weekend, Randy and I got drunk. At the time, I thought I was just having fun.

But the "fun" didn't stop there. By the time it did stop, fun had been replaced with a living hell.

CHAPTER 4
DEEPER WATER

Randy went on to college, so that meant for the first time since I was 10, I had to start making friends my own age. So I did. As a natural-born bullshitter, I could talk to anyone, especially with a drink to bolster my confidence. I started drinking more. Not enough to be drunk or obnoxious—just enough to get through social awkwardness. But as I poured more alcohol on my low self esteem, the social awkwardness grew, too.

It got to the point where I had a drink or two in me at all times.

A couple of my new friends, Kurt and Phil, went to the house of another friend, Davis. We were hanging out doing nothing in particular. Then Phil's older brother, Skyler, showed up with some of his friends.

"Hey," Skyler asked. "Wanna try something that will blow your mind?"

He pulled out a bag of white powder: cocaine—the same drug that would eventually kill Davis by overdose.

We were kids, and we were stupid. As a natural risk-taker, I needed no convincing. I was in. Before long, Kurt and Phil wanted in, too.

"Five bucks," Skyler said, snapping his fingers and showing the "give-me" sign with his hand. "Each."

We ponied up the money.

That night, Kurt, Phil, and I split 1/4 gram of cocaine. We each did a line.

It was love at first snort. It gave me energy, even focus. My mind seemed to work better. Doing so poorly in school, I always felt like an outsider, an outcast. But when I drank, and now with a snootful of cocaine, my tongue loosened up. I could talk. I always had the gift of gab, but now I felt like a real, whole person. I felt... normal for the first time in my life. I fit in with these older kids and was cool, accepted as an equal, and not the dumbest kid in the class. I was self medicating, and I didn't know it.

After my friends left, I pulled Skyler aside. "Dude, what's it going to take to score some more of that?" I asked.

"Here's what I'll do for you," Skyler said, thinking for a short moment. "I have a half gram left. I'll split it with you. But you've got to pay me $25 on Friday. Deal?"

"Hell, yeah!" I said before he changed his mind. "That's a no brainer. Let's do it. I'll bring you my lunch money."

Before long, my growing habit was costing me more than lunch money.

Unless you lived through the early '80s, you probably can't imagine cocaine's allure. It made average-looking people feel attractive, introverted people feel outgoing. Cocaine seemed glamorous, and it was glorified in movies like *Scarface*. Yeah, I know that in the movie everyone dies in the end, but that would never happen to me. I was *too* smart for that.

I kept water skiing. That was my ticket to a better life, I knew. But I started to check out of other things. Like school. Instead of trying to learn, I spent Monday through Friday's class time planning the weekend party. I spent every waking hour figuring out how to score booze and cocaine.

Cocaine started to deplete my pocketbook. By junior year, I would pick up seven grams of coke. I would cut the hell out of it, go to parties, and try to make just enough money that my own lines cost me nothing. But I snorted more than I made. I'd make $300 a paycheck, and it would be gone every Friday night.

Cocaine chipped away at my ability to hold a relationship. I'd be on a date with a really smart, beautiful girl who was really into me. What more could a horny high school boy want, right? Cocaine, that's what. More than once, I'd end the date early because the need for cocaine was greater than my need for affection or friendship.

I had tickets to see Pink Floyd when they were the hottest band around. I bailed, because I wasn't willing to go to the concert without cocaine, and I was too broke to score any.

Internal conflict started early—this battle to balance between two worlds: party animal and school, party animal and water skiing fanatic. Later, I would battle between party animal and businessman, and party animal and family man. Eventually, the conflict stopped. It stopped because the party animal won.

Having a boat on Crystal Lake, everyone flocked to our house. Our home became a revolving door of people. I had one simple rule for hanging out with me: bring gas for my boat or beer for my belly. Simple as that. No free rides.

During the school the year, I'd go on these weekend benders, doing cocaine 24/7. I'd stay up all night and watch the sun rise. Then I'd come home and act like everything was fine, when in reality I could barely stay awake—or my eyes were stuck open and popping halfway out of my head.

My parents weren't suspicious by nature. But at times, they had good reason to question me. One of my good friends, a guy named Jake, stole some gold Krugerrands from another mutual friend for cocaine money. Jake went to treatment shortly after that. When he got out, my mom asked him, "Jake, do we need to worry about Tim?"

"Oh hell, yeah," Jake told her. "Tim does coke with me all of the time." That was it. My parents took me to a place called The Arc, a drug treatment center located in Hoffman Estates. The staff planned to check me in. Then I did what all addicts do: I lied. I lied like my freedom depended on it, because it did.

And it worked. The intake people didn't admit me.

My bullshit kept working. For a while. But I knew that I couldn't keep playing this game the same way, so I laid low for a while. I even wrote my parents a note to reassure them that I was a changed young man:

> *I Timothy M Ryan will never again from this day*
>
> *on 3/12/86 take any type of drug, and limit my beer*
>
> *drinking down to a six pack when I go out unless*
>
> *special occasion (graduation etc if I make it) and*
>
> *if I violate this I must get help or it is by by tim hello*
>
> *crule world.*

My mom recently sent me the original, handwritten note that she'd kept all of these years. It proved two things. First, I was already an addict in 1986. No doubt about it. The scheming and conniving manipulation pours out of that note. Second, addicts lie. I used my legal name and the correct date. The rest of it was total bullshit, and I knew it even as I wrote it.

Oh, did you notice the lack of punctuation and horrible spelling? No, I am not making it up when I say that I suffered from learning disabilities. That was my finest writing.

Of course, after I wrote that note, I was a good boy for a few days. But it wasn't long before things went back to normal. Well, what I called normal. Meaning nothing changed.

CHAPTER 5
HIT THAT, MAN

Finally, and not because I earned it, I finished high school. I applied at several colleges, and as I said, only two accepted me: Southern Illinois and Northeast Louisiana University (which is now called University of Louisiana at Monroe). But I wasn't built for school. I wanted to have fun instead. So a buddy and I decided to move to Hawaii where we could be beach bums, hang around beautiful girls, and ski year-round. I packed my things and bought a plane ticket. But the night before we were set to leave, something changed my mind.

"Dad, I'm not going to Hawaii," I told him. "I'm going to college—Northeast Louisiana University."

I picked Louisiana for three strategic reasons: they had the best girl to guy ratio in the country (3:1), they had an intercollegiate water ski team, we could hunt and fish all day long, and the drinking age was 18 (compared to 21 in Illinois). Okay, that's four. Have I told you I'm not great at math?

"Great!" my dad spoke sincerely. "I'm really glad to hear that. And I'm glad you have enough money to keep you afloat the first few months." I guess he thought when I said I was saving money for college that I hadn't been snorting every last dollar up my nose like I'd actually done.

My mom flew down to school with me, and I couldn't wait for her to leave so I could run to the liquor store. Once she left, I made a bee-line to buy a six-pack of Bartles & James, a case of beer, and a bottle of Jim Beam. Inside two hours, I was piss drunk.

Once I sobered up, I thought, *Oh shit. Time to make some cash.* This became my pattern for the next several years: make money; blow it on alcohol and drugs; repeat.

I got a job at T.J. Cinnamon Bun for $2.25 an hour making cinnamon rolls. I would intentionally burn some, so I could take them home and eat them. I wasn't about to waste money on food. I needed all of my cash for booze.

My roommate, Bodie, was on the water ski team. I met a couple of other guys who would become my go-to guys for the next couple of years: Jacob and Tad. They were fellow NLU students, and they were locals. These two Southern boys taught me to catch crayfish, go muddin', and shoot guns. Of course, they didn't need to teach me to drink or water ski; I had those mastered.

For the first few months, I didn't have a worry in the world.

I got into hallucinogenics, starting with shrooms. Magic mushrooms grew wild down there, and I could pick my own for nothing.

Tad introduced me to acid. He lived on a bayou with his dad, Wylie. Another buddy, Jacob, lived across the street with his mom. Wylie was a divorced, high end accountant, and he let us do whatever the hell we wanted. He'd ask us to drive him to a social club, where he'd play poker and get pig drunk. And he'd pay us $100 to pick him up, so he wouldn't get a DUI. Of course, when Tad and I picked him up, all of us were three sheets to the wind.

I lived in a never-ending party. From sun up to sun down, I did nothing but party, hunt, fish, and chase women. Yeah, like I'm going to class when I'm making enough money to score drugs and women. I may have been stupid, but I was no dummy.

I started hanging out with members of the Phi Beta Sigma fraternity, because many of them were from Chicago. One day when I was slamming drinks with these guys, one of them named Jasper said, "I got something for you to try, Tim. Follow me."

I followed him to his dorm room. He took some white rocks, put it in baby food jar he'd converted into a free-base crack pipe, and lit it.

"Hit that, man, and hold that smoke in deep," Jasper told me.

As much as I loved pure, white powder cocaine, I loved rock cocaine's brother—better known as "crack"—even more. It hit me much more quickly. Within 30 seconds, I was through the roof. Crack served as a short stop before trying methamphetamine and crystal meth. And then I discovered Ecstasy.

A year earlier, Ecstasy had been legal in the state of Texas, and plenty of it was still available. A couple of buddies and I went into business running X. During the week, we'd drive to Mississippi, pick up $10,000 in cash from the guy who fronted us the money, drive to Houston, and then buy 10,000 hits of Ecstasy for a buck a piece. We'd drive back to Mississippi to pay back our money man with his pills. He'd pay us back with interest in both cash and pills, since we were assuming most of the risk. I would sell those pills for $15 to $20 each. I wasn't great at math, but by my calculations, this was easy money.

When money got tight, I'd get another job. I found that I loved selling. For a time, I sold Electrolux vacuum cleaners door to door with a really interesting man, Brent Johnson. Brent was 62, and he was helping his dad, Lloyd Johnson, who was 85 or older. For these two, experienced guys, selling expensive vacuum cleaners to poor people was as easy as shooting fish in a barrel.

In his 62 years Brent had done it all—smuggling drugs, working on oil rigs, and managing both Jimi Hendrix and Janis Joplin. And no, I didn't believe him either, until he showed me the pictures. He fascinated me. And his dad, Lloyd, was a kick, too. The first time I met him, he pulled up to the office and popped the hood of his 1972 Cadillac.

"You got car problems, old timer?" I asked, moving to the front of the car—like I had any idea what I'd do if he answered, "Yes."

"Nope," he said, taking a rectangular shaped roll of tin foil off the manifold. "Egg sandwich. Cooked perfectly, just the way I like it."

What made selling so easy is that I had no problem lying. We worked in teams. Lloyd or Brent worked the machine. That was our strategy. They were old. No one likes to see the elderly doing door-to-door sales work when it's hotter than hell outside. My role was the pitch to get inside that house, and it went something like this:

"Hey, I wonder if you could help us out. I'm trying to get scholarship money so I can go to college. I get $10 if all you do is let us come in and show you how this vacuum works. Can you please just let us show you? It'll only take a few minutes." Of course all of that was a lie. I was a far cry from a college scholarship contender, and I got nothing if they just let me in the door. But I stood to gain a lot more than $10 if I could get one of them to buy.

These were families in northern Louisiana and southern Arkansas who didn't make 15 grand a year, and here we were trying to sell them a $2,000 vacuum. Well, once we got inside, we'd do this thing where we'd vacuum the top of the mattress and show them on a clean filter all of the shit that came out of the bed they were sleeping on.

"Wow," I'd say. "Can you believe all of THAT is in your mattress? And it looks so clean, too. That's how good this vacuum cleaner is." Blah blah blah.

People would go for it. Hell, it was good vacuum. But $2,000 good? Once we hooked them, we'd help them finance it. It sounds insane that we helped them finance a $2,000 vacuum, doesn't it? My take: $250. Enough for a couple good hours of partying.

A guy who later became a well-known country music star went to my school. He was in the Pi Kappa Alpha fraternity, known as Pikes. He played guitar every Wednesday night at a local café. We once got talking about our families. He said that his life had been touched by addiction, too. He was embarrassed by some of his family history and didn't want the stigma of addiction to stick to him. I saw that, but at the time, it didn't really make sense to me.

If you get a hole in the bottom of your boat, the last thing you should do is put another hole in it to let the water out. That shit doesn't work. But that's what I was doing with my money and drug use. When I made more money, I did more drugs; when I made less money, I still did more drugs.

I didn't have a money problem. I had a drug problem.

As the party rocked, I stood in the center of it, full of life. But when the lights went out, shame surrounded me. *How the fuck do I spend every fucking penny on cocaine?* I cursed my weakness without being ready to acknowledge it. I just knew it really bothered me. So when I didn't have money for coke, I drank. Booze, I could afford.

Finally, the money came to an end. Which didn't matter, because I'd flunked out of all of my classes anyway. Something would have to give.

CHAPTER 6

UP IN SMOKE

I took a semester off and worked construction in Chicago. The work was hard. Even if you didn't drink, you'd want to drink to numb your soreness at the end of the day.

One day, I was working alongside Thad James, a 35-year-old from Marengo, Illinois. We were digging a ditch or some backbreaking job that required frequent breaks.

We sat chugging water when Thad spoke up, "Tim, I'm 35 years old." I was 18 or 19 at the time. Thad continued, "My back's shot, my knees are shot. This kind of work chews you up and spits you out broken."

"Yeah," I said, not knowing what to say. "I've only been doing this a few weeks, and I already hate it."

"Get the hell out of here. Go back to college."

Thad had a great heart. He was telling me something out of love. I listened.

I'd been saving money to go back to school. I quit work and headed back to Louisiana.

When I got back to Monroe, I had $3,000 on me. I smoked $3,000 in crack and was penniless in five days. I couldn't help myself. I tried school for one more semester but failed again.

Broke and more ashamed than ever, I returned to Crystal Lake, where I moved in with my parents. I vowed to stay away from drugs, because they were breaking me. I got a job at Fretter's selling stereo equipment, TVs, and refrigerators. I was a good salesman. I'd learned the basics in Louisiana, and it came easy to me.

But it wasn't long before a couple of guys at work invited me to join them in a few snorts. And bam. It was like I never stopped.

Right after that, I went to a party with some old high school friends. Michelle McCormick and Haley Dean came into the bedroom, where I still had white powder all over my nose. "Tim, you're gonna die. You need help. You're just out of control with this." They tried to reason with me.

Yeah, yeah, yeah. Fuck it. Fuck them.

When I didn't have cocaine, I was an asshole. So I kept working hard enough to make enough money so that I would always have coke.

That's when I met a guy, Sean, who was probably 20 years older than me. He was my connect. We'd go to Chicago every day and get an ounce of cocaine. He was getting it through the Columbians at the time. Sean would meet this old Columbian lady at a church every day. The lady was very pious, extremely religious. She sold cocaine, sure, no problem. But she wouldn't use it. Hell, *that* would be a sin. What kind of crazy belief system would say it's okay to sell drugs but not to use them?

I was raised Catholic and forced to go to CCD (Cofraternity of Christian Doctrine—prep for Confirmation). That makes me a recovering Catholic, I guess. As a kid, I was dragged to church, kicking and screaming. None of it made sense to me. I'd do something wrong, and I'd have to go to confession. Then I'd go tell the priest all about my crimes. He'd say, "Okay, say five Hail Marys, say five Our Fathers, and you're good to go."

Hell, this shit is great, I thought. I can screw around all week, say some magic words, and I'm good again. But then I'd hear another message like, "You're going to Hell for all of the rotten things you've done!"

Wait a minute! The priest just told me that everything was cool between me and God, so what's this Hell thing?

God became this boogie man who confused me. Is He good and forgiving? Or is He vengeful, someone to fear, and the guy who would throw me into Hell?

So you know how I ended up coming to peace with my first spiritual dilemma? My parents would drop us off in front of the church, and I would ditch out and shoot pinball over at Pinemoor Pizza. Then I'd come back for church and sit there all smiles. Tommy never told on us. Yeah, the way I saw it, religion was for crazy people.

Fast-forward 10 years, and I was walking into a Catholic church to buy cocaine from "church lady." All of the holy water and crucifixes in the world couldn't keep me from getting what I needed. What the hell did I care?

Sean and I would get an ounce, come back, sell half, and smoke the rest. I was smoking a half ounce of cocaine a day and spending all my paychecks just to supply my coke.

I needed more money. So I started stealing checks from my mom. At my buddy's gas station, I could go in and cash checks, $200 to $300, whatever. And it would go right up my nose.

The shame grew stronger. The wheels started falling off my party wagon. I didn't want to do this anymore. I was ready to get some help.

I called a drug treatment center called Parkside Lodge in Mundelein, Illinois. Without telling anyone, I drove myself there and tried to check myself in. They had me sit in their small group with about 40 people, while they tried to run my dad's insurance. They were having a hard time getting ahold of my mom or dad.

I started jonesing. I felt the wad of cash in my pocket: $400.

"Um, yeah," I stood up in the group. "I don't think this is for me." I walked out.

I spent the $400 on a hard bender. Once I snorted through that, I stole a check from my brother, Sam, for another $400.

My friend at the gas station knew it was time to intervene. He called my mom. "Hey, Tim's got a problem," he told her. "He's deep into cocaine. He's here trying to cash a check of Sam's for $400, and he's going to buy more blow with it."

That's when the shit hit the fan.

I wanted to get help. I didn't want to live like this anymore. I said, "All right. I'll go. I'm ready to get help."

My little brother drove me back to the Parkside Lodge. That was 1990. I was ready to turn over a new leaf. But first, I bought Cameron a case of beer for his trouble. I drank eight of them before I got out of the car to enter treatment.

Lying in bed that first night, I thought a lot about God. Not the God of my childhood. Certainly not the God whose house in Chicago was used to sell drugs. The God I thought about was the God of Maggie Baker, a beautiful little Christian girl I had met in college.

Maggie was from Vicksburg, Mississippi. She was drop-dead gorgeous, and the nicest, sweetest girl I had ever known. We met in one of our classes. I can't remember the exact semester, but I remember we started dating.

Of course, I ultimately blew that. She wanted me to go to church with her on a Wednesday night, and I was like, "*Who goes to church on Wednesday night?*" I just couldn't wrap my head around that. *I mean, are you kidding me? I'll tell you where I'm going. I'm going to Freddies because it's $5 all-you-can-drink night. That's where I'm going.*

I ruined that relationship because of my drinking and drugging. I had no off switch.

And Maggie? She had something I had never seen before. She had a relationship with God, is what she had. Closing my eyes that night, I wondered if I'd ever meet Him.

CHAPTER 7
A TEMPORARY REPRIEVE

Let me be clear about my expectations for treatment: I *did* want help—to learn how to drink and take drugs like "normal" people. That's it. I didn't want to be a teetotaler. In my mind, if I had a problem, it was that I couldn't handle my drugs and alcohol very well.

Parkside Lodge was a beautiful place. There were 38 of us as clients. Eleven were Chicago cops.

The wheels started turning for me. I attended groups. I listened. I even shared some of my struggles with the other clients. I started eating again—real food. In 30 days, I put on 30 pounds. I started feeling good.

I learned something: if you want to find out how many friends you have, go to drug treatment. Outside of my mom and dad, only two friends visited. I should have recognized that fact for what it was: I didn't have many real friends. Instead, I had good times friends, people who were nice when I had a bag of something they wanted. But they wouldn't cross the street to piss on me if I were on fire.

Before I entered Parkside Lodge, I'd planned to move to Austria with my best friend at the time, a guy named Eric. He played pro hockey for Austria. I got my passport and told everyone that I was off to Europe. But in the back of my mind, I knew if I went, I'd die. I was out of control. As much I'd become a selfish asshole, I didn't want to take down Eric's career.

A few weeks before we would leave the country, we did cocaine at his parents' house. Eric snorted one line and said, "My God! I like this." His eyes got big, and he sucked in a deep breath. His next words surprised me: "I'll never do it again."

Who the hell says that? I wondered to myself. I mean, he clearly loved it. Why would he never do it again?

A person who doesn't want to become an addict, that's who.

The next day, Eric and I went camping with another buddy, Brock. We had a blast and were ready to drop. Having good common sense, Eric crawled into his tent, zipped it closed, and announced, "I'm going to bed. Don't keep me up all night."

So what do you think Brock and I did? We snorted cocaine all night and knocked down a fifth of whiskey.

Just as the sun started to pop up, Eric stuck his head out of his tent. "What the hell are you idiots doing? Why are you up?" Eric shook his head in disgust.

"What do you mean?" I laughed. "We're doing cocaine, what do you think?"

I might as well have spoken Klingon to him. Eric couldn't understand why Brock and I were so stupid. And Brock and I couldn't wrap our heads around how Eric said he'd never do cocaine again and meant it. I was a mess. Eric knew it. My family knew it. And I knew it.

I didn't go to Europe. I went to drug treatment instead.

My parents came to every family group. My uncle, who I always looked up to, told my folks that he planned to visit. I couldn't wait. He never showed. As petty as it sounds, it hurt me.

Besides my parents and a couple of friends, Parkside Lodge opened its doors to a bunch of strangers to keep us company and teach us recovery. I got into it. Listening to their stories, I felt like maybe they *got me.* They all talked about how drugs and/or booze had made their lives unmanageable. And they shared something else: they all had entered active recovery.

One guy shared his story and then looked around the room slowly before saying something I'll never forget: "Only one of you will be sober a year from now." My mind and body were clear for the first time in years, because I'd stopped poisoning myself with chemicals that impaired my reasoning. I spoke up immediately, while the others in the group sat in silence.

"Excuse me, sir, what did you say?" Arrogance rang in my voice, as if my couple of weeks of sober living gave me the expertise to challenge this guy. "There are 38 of us here."

He dropped his eyes into mine, held my gaze, and said, "Kid, listen to me, one of you will be sober in a year."

I squirmed in my chair. "What do I do?" *If what this guy says is true, what can I do to increase my odds of being the one in 38?* I wondered.

"Don't drink, and go to those 12-step meetings."

"Ok, great," I smiled nervously and a little confused. I'd expected to find some big secret weapon or magic spell I could use to give me an advantage. But what this guy said made one thing clear: recovery started with me.

And as long as I was in treatment, I was game with doing the work. I ate and slept well, didn't drink, and faithfully attended every group meeting.

When my discharge date approached, I told myself that I was ready, that I would take my recovery very seriously.

When I got out, my parents also made it clear that they were taking my recovery very seriously. My dad sat me down right after I got home. Pain pulled at the corners of his face, but I wasn't ready to accept that I was any part of its cause.

"Tim, your mom and I have been doing a lot of thinking, a lot of trying to process."

"Process what?" I asked defensively. "What are you thinking?"

"We're wondering…I'm wondering," my dad said with sorrow I didn't understand, "Where did I go wrong? What did I do as a parent? Tim, I can't sleep, I'm so worried about you."

By that time, my dad had worked up the ranks at E.F. Hutton to the level of senior vice president. He ran the whole country. He was no slacker, and his mind was incredibly sharp. When he made up his mind about something, it wasn't on a whim. He'd done his homework as well as his soul-searching to come up with some decision. I just didn't yet know what it was.

"So I've been going to some meetings of my own: Al-Anon," he told me. "And they got to me, son."

I looked up to see his eyes grow a little wider, like he had something important to say—maybe something a little awkward. "Okay. How'd they get to you?"

My dad looked me directly in the eyes. I saw a mixture of shame and determination.

"Tim, I didn't cause your disease. I can't cure it, I can't control it, and I sure as shit will not contribute to it," he said as if he'd been rehearsing those words. Turns out, he had. And not just once or twice.

"So," he continued, "you're welcome to stay with us on a couple of conditions. First, keep going to meetings. Second, the day you drink or do drugs, you're out. And then you can figure it all out on your own, but not here, not in this home."

Ironically, as I sat there listening to his speech, I was finally legal to drink. I had turned 21 in September. On my 21st birthday, I was at Southside Johnny's Bar in Crystal Lake celebrating, and the bartender/owner came up and said, "So what birthday is this for you, Tim? You 24 or 25?"

"I'm 21."

"21? Are you shittin' me? You've been coming in here for four years."

"Yeah, I know."

"Well, happy birthday, you son-of-a-bitch. Have a shot on the house. You really pulled one over on me."

I always tried to fit in with older people, and that's probably why others saw me as older than I was.

So as I sat listening to my father, the greatest man I knew, and even though I was 21 and finally legally old enough to drink, I realized that to meet my dad's expectations, I had to stay clean and sober.

"You've got a deal, Dad," I told him as I gave him a hug.

And I meant it.

I started going to 12-step meetings at the Alano Club in Crystal Lake. I loved them—but not so much for the recovery part. I loved playing cards with some of the old guys attending meetings there. Truthfully, I still didn't understand the program.

So what is this program all about? I wondered. *You read through these 12 steps and a few pages of a book, you share what's on your mind, and you drink coffee with a bunch of other people who don't want to drink. Is that recovery?*

Around that time, I met Judd and Blake Rollins who owned a big asphalt sealcoating business. They had been so successful on the commercial side of the business that they wanted to sell off the residential side. Since I needed a job, I was interested.

"Mom, I want to buy a residential asphalt business," I announced.

A few hours later, my mom and I walked into the bank and

spoke with the branch president.

"How much do you want?" asked the man in the navy blue pinstriped suit and red power tie.

"$10,000," I replied. That might seem like a lot to most 21-year-olds, but I was used to seeing cash flow through my hands like water. I knew that if I could go through that amount of money in days doing drugs, I could probably earn it in days, too, if I put my heart into it and didn't snort it all up my nose.

"Sign here," he said, handing me a document before cutting a check for 10 grand.

With that money, I bought two pickup trucks and my own asphalt sealcoating business that I called Ryan Sealcoat Specialists.

I started making money right away. Life was good. To make it better, Mike Frankenbush opened Walking on Water Ski School and asked me if I wanted a piece of his business. I partnered with him. Before long, I got hard core back into barefoot water skiing.

So at 21 years old, I finally had my shit together. I was running my own sealcoating business, teaching water skiing, and attending 12-step meetings—which really just meant drinking a lot of coffee and playing cards.

I promised my dad that I would stay clean, so one day I decided that instead of just attending meetings and going through the motions that maybe I should actually start to work the steps and find a sponsor. I raised my hand in a meeting. "Yeah, I'm Tim. I'm an alcoholic. I'm looking for a sponsor."

Nobody responded. I mean, nobody said anything to me during the meeting or even afterwards. Months passed. I still went to the meetings. But I had asked for a sponsor, and nobody came forward. I got resentful. *What the hell is wrong with these people?*

About six months later, this big guy came up to me as I was complaining to someone that I couldn't find a sponsor to help me.

"Excuse me, son," he said. "I've got to tell you something. You, son, are the stupidest person I've ever met."

"What are you talking about?" I felt intense anger brewing for the first time in months. I'd always felt stupid, but who the hell was this fat, stupid, son-of-a-bitch to call me stupid to my face?

"No one's gonna just *be* your sponsor. It's like dating. You gotta go ask someone."

"Oh," I said, calming down. "Well, nobody told me that."

When I left that day, I played the tapes of that encounter over in my head, and I felt my resentment growing. *Those SOBs tell you to go to meetings*, I thought. *But no one explains how this shit works. How am I supposed to know that I've got to ask someone? This is ridiculous. And who the hell was that guy to call me stupid?*

What started as a little pebble of resentment grew into a mountain of bitterness by the end of the day. I quit going to meetings.

But so what? Life was still great. I started training hard, and by the end of the season, I was the barefoot water skiing champion of Illinois, Michigan, and Wisconsin. Sponsorship offers poured in. Could my life get any better?

I knew if I placed well at the Midwest Regionals, I could sell the sealcoating business and focus full time on the water skiing school. With sponsorship, I would have money hand-over-fist for doing the one thing I truly loved and was gifted at.

Fate had another plan. During the competition, I took a nasty fall and blew out three disks in my lower back.

The fall into the cool water was nothing compared to my emotional plunge. I felt irrelevant. The one thing I was good at, I could no longer do. My barefoot water skiing career was over. And with it, my resolve to stay clean and sober sunk like a rock in that lake.

CHAPTER 8
TWO STEPS FORWARD, THREE STEPS BACK

Bitterness consumed me like acid. Some stranger had called me stupid, and an accident had taken away the only thing I loved. My resentments grew. I got more pissed by the day.

Brock and I went to a Grateful Dead concert. A guy was selling stuff out of the back of his VW van. I looked inside in the direction of a poster he was selling.

"For you," the dead-head salesman said with a silky voice, "the poster is $7. And I'll throw in a fatty," he said, pointing to a thick marijuana joint lying in front of the poster.

"I want that poster, man," I told Brock.

I can't tell you what was on that poster. Shit, I hadn't even seen the damned poster. I stopped because I saw that joint. I was going to have it.

"No, man, you don't want that joint." Brock laughed at me. "Just say 'No.'" Even though he was laughing, his words showed me genuine concern.

"Dude, one joint will be fine," I said. "One."

Brock knew me better. *I* knew me better.

Very quickly, I was right back to drinking and doing cocaine.

Nothing changed.

I moved out of my parents' house. They knew that I had failed, and I didn't want to look at their disappointed faces. I moved into an apartment. The asphalt business was seasonal. As winter hit,

I started working for a buddy selling cars at his dealership just to make rent.

But after a short time, I had the same problem I'd had many times before: pay rent, or buy drugs. Which do you think I did?

Yeah, I quit paying the rent and got evicted.

I needed a change of scenery, maybe some place that wasn't so damned cold and depressing. So I moved to Austin, Texas, to live with a childhood friend of mine, Tracen. My boy Tracen was smart. He'd just graduated from UT and already owned a house. He was so smart that he'd converted the house into three apartments so he could make extra money. We stayed on one side, and he rented out another unit to a country Western singer. She strummed her guitar and put me to sleep every night. Her rent checks came from MCA Records. She is still a big name artist.

Tracen ran a landscaping business and worked an office job at the same time. And me? I did a couple of odd jobs, attended an occasional 12-step program in a very half-assed fashion, and smoked weed. In other words, I putzed around and leeched off my friend.

I got the itch to use drugs in a real way again. Not pot. I itched for something really good. I flipped on the news. A reporter announced someone had gotten shot on 13th Street.

"I'm going to 13th Street," I told Tracen as I headed out with his truck keys in my hands and his cell phone in my pocket. If someone got shot on 13th Street, there were drugs on 13th Street.

Once there, I traded Tracen's cell phone for crack. Later, when he noticed his phone missing, I suggested that some asshole probably stole it.

Since my stay in that treatment center, I knew I had a problem with drugs and alcohol. I knew that while some people—like Eric—could take it or leave it, I quickly lost the ability to "leave it" once I started using again.

But I told myself that I was not back to square one. Even though I was pissed off by my bad experience at a meeting when a guy called me stupid, I still attended them occasionally. I figured maybe something would stick if I just showed up enough times. It's funny, sitting in class in high school didn't help me absorb whatever the hell the teacher was dishing out. So I'm not sure why I believed that rubbing against people in recovery would somehow transfer recovery to me, but I think part of me believed it would.

One thing did rub off on me from the meetings: the relationships I built. I met a couple of go-getter types. They sold cable television door to door, and to hear them tell it, they made a killing.

Maybe these meetings had value after all, I thought. Networking! I started working with these guys, and pretty soon I mastered a whole new level of salesmanship. I'd start my day in a meeting, work my ass off selling cable by day, and spend my nights smoking crack and other drugs until morning.

As usual, it didn't matter how much money I made, I always sent more up in smoke than I could bring in. As Christmas approached, I wanted to do something nice for Tracen. I mean, this guy took me in, let me leech off him while I did next to nothing, and never accused me of stealing—even though I'd ripped him off to fund my drug addiction since I'd moved in.

All I had to show for my growing financial success was blackened teeth and crack-breath. So I decided to get creative. I knew Tracen had great credit, so I copied down all of his personal info, visited a local Circuit City, and filled out a credit application as Tracen. "My" great credit earned me a $1,500 line that I could use immediately. I bought two video cameras: one for $1,000 and another for $450. I never opened them. Instead, I drove to the closest pawn shop and sold them for $350.

I was such a great guy that I headed straight to the Harley dealer, where I bought Tracen a custom-made Harley buck knife. I even got a little something for his girlfriend. Oh, and then I spent the rest on a little something for me: drugs.

Don't get me wrong. My intention was not to be a rotten son-of-a-bitch to my closest friend. I just wanted to do something nice. I thought: *Well, I'm working now. I make good money. I'll get the money, pay this off, and he'll never know.*

I forgot about a bill getting mailed to Tracen's house. A few weeks passed. I came home from selling cable one day, and Tracen was on the porch with all of my stuff packed. He was crying real tears.

"How could you do this to me?"

When Tracen was 9, he was in a car accident with his mom, and she didn't survive. His dad wasn't in his life at the time. Tracen's grandparents were great people, and they stepped in to raise him. He was sent to boarding schools when he wasn't spending time on his family's ranch with his grandparents.

At 14, his dad resurfaced with a new wife and two new kids. Tracen felt like a second-hand son. I met Tracen through his father, who knew my father. I became his family. He trusted me. He became my brother, the brother I hoped I would never screw over—but I did.

Tracen kicked me out, and I didn't think my life could get any worse.

It did. A couple of days later, while selling cable at a gas station, I got arrested—charged with theft and forgery. They hauled me off to Travis County Jail.

Not only had Tracen thrown me out, but he'd taken it a step further and turned me in.

This wasn't my first arrest. Once in Louisiana, I got pinched for stealing a pack of cigarettes, but I got bailed out right away. No big deal. But here I was alone in the huge state of Texas, where Tracen, the only person I really knew, had just gotten me arrested. So it wasn't like I could turn around and call him for bail money.

After they processed me, the police put me in a two-man cell with four rough looking guys. I could do drugs with the toughest of guys, because we shared an objective; but sitting in a cell with them terrified me.

I called my mom to plead for help, but Tracen had already called her. He was like family, remember? Yeah, he threw me out and got me arrested. But that didn't mean he wanted me to rot in jail.

"Tim, listen." I could tell Mom had a mission, and relief flooded me. "Do you remember a babysitter of yours named Margaret Burns? Well, she moved to Austin several years ago. And today she works for the assistant state's attorney. I'll call her and see what she can do."

Next thing I knew, I got bailed out.

As soon as I could, I hightailed out of Texas for Michigan. I figured with the cable business experience I'd gotten in Texas, I could go anywhere I wanted and write my own ticket. Some of the guys selling cable moved to Michigan with me. They were all in recovery, and for the most part, these were good guys who really worked the program. Coming off my latest legal problems in Texas (which I knew that drugs played a huge part in), I started working on getting clean and sober again.

And it worked. As my mind got healthier, my pocketbook got fatter. My team and I started knocking on doors all over Houghton Lake, a region around 40 minutes east of Cadillac,

Michigan. Business was gangbusters! Cable was new, and everyone wanted it. It wasn't heavily regulated, so we could cut deals to put the most money in our pockets, which was good for us. But we also put money in the cable company's pockets, which was great for them.

Six months later, my boss asked me if I would go to Buffalo, New York, to be a manager.

Hell yeah! Two weeks later, I was growing my business in Buffalo, where I hired 20 new salespeople. One of the guys I hired, Eddie, had just gone through a divorce. He was still feeling kind of raw, so he asked me if I would bring some presents to his ex-wife for their kids so he wouldn't have to see her just yet.

No problem. I knocked on the door and delivered the gifts to Eddie's ex-wife, Tasha, who seemed like a nice lady. I didn't think much of it. My team reached new heights for sales, and that made us in high demand. Our crew got called to go all over the country for three to six month bids. The company knew that a good sales team could cherry-pick 80 percent of immediately interested cable customers before the competition ever got to town. My life had gone from great to crap many times over again, but finally I found myself in a good, stable place. In the back of my head somewhere, it's like I heard that old TV ad playing in my mind: *"It's Miller time."*

Normal people don't understand that recovering addicts often relapse when times are great—not just when things get shitty. When you're jobless, friendless, and sitting in a holding cell, using just takes you down further; when you're at the bottom, you can only go so far. Success can make recovering addicts feel like they've earned a big celebration. That's when they get lazy and arrogant about their recovery. And that's when they slip.

That's when I slipped.

CHAPTER 9
WHAT ADDICTS DO BEST

It was in this frame of mind that I made my way down to South Florida, where I reconnected with Josh Crenshaw, my former water ski coach, who was a world champion. I let my team do the work I had trained them for, while I took a little break helping Josh train the British barefoot water ski team. I was in my element. Things went so well that I trained the French, Australian, and Canadian teams, too. I was good at it, and I loved being outside. Once again, I earned cash for something I loved.

Josh's friend from California came for a visit. She and I hit it off immediately, because we had a couple of things in common: we both liked getting drunk and having sex. What started off as a glass of wine here and a little groping in the backseat there developed into regular drunken sex for the duration of her visit to Florida.

By the time her vacation was over, she told me something I didn't expect to hear. "I know we just met, but I'm falling in love with you," she gushed like a teenager. "I want to buy you a ticket to California. Come back with me. I think we could have something wonderful."

Boom, here's my ticket outta here, I thought but didn't say. I'd been working hard, I told myself. And, having gotten my beak wet again with alcohol, I craved even more excitement. I was ready for a change of scenery.

"I love you, too," I lied. "Wow! I can't believe that this has finally happened to me. Fate, huh?"

We flew to California, where I got a couple of jobs to make quick cash. In the meantime, my new "girlfriend" and I had great sex while drinking ourselves silly on her tab.

My former manager in New York was trying to track me down, and we finally connected on the phone. "Tim, we could use you here. Why don't you come back to Buffalo and start your own business? Business is HOT, and there's a lot of money waiting to be made."

Boom! I was done in California anyway. I'd been living it up and partying on this lady's dime. It was time to move on. Finally, I'd saved enough cash to leave town—with a job opportunity to boot. I dumped her cold, like only an addict—or asshole—could do.

It didn't matter to me. I'd had my fun. I'd gotten what I wanted out of her: a trip to California, a drinking buddy, quick cash, and unlimited affection. Now I was done with her.

I headed back to Buffalo, and the first person I called was one of the only people I knew in town, Tasha, my employee Eddie's ex-wife.

"Hey, you," she said excitedly. "Come on by! I'd love to see you and welcome you back to Buffalo!"

I knocked on her door with a smile and a bottle of Captain Morgan. And I stayed. She had two little kids, Rob and Patrick, who were two and four. Eddie had disappeared from the picture, so that helped ease my guilt…if I'd had any. Which I didn't.

To start a business, I needed startup capital. So I harnessed skills I'd developed as an addict: I lied, begged, borrowed, and stole enough to scrape together $15,000 for short-term payroll. I started TR Enterprises International Limited, my own cable marketing company. Within six months, I had 60 people working for me, and I was bringing in $20,000 to $25,000 a week, free and clear profit. Any money that was left over after paying at least some of the bills was spent on an over $1,000-dollar-a-day cocaine habit.

Even when I had no money, I still found a way to score drugs. But when I had lots of money, I just scored more and better drugs.

My partying intensified with Tasha. We both had an insatiable appetite for cocaine, and my full monster ran unleashed. The cocaine made me feel super-human and powerful. I had energy, drive, and more cash than I could spend. I developed new business projects in California, Ohio, Wisconsin, and Illinois. I was flying around with suitcases filled with $10,000 in cash like a mini mobster.

While working at sobriety in Parkside Lodge, I didn't have any friends. But as an addict, I was a rock star surrounded by people who had my back, especially when it came to getting high. On a flight to California, Tasha's voice crackled over the in-flight phone: "Check your wallet. I packed some acid in there for you." What a woman.

When I landed, I connected with a buddy, and we drove through Beverly Hills tripping on acid. We were bulletproof. We pulled into mansions and swam in pools. It's the kind of thing you see in movies, and it makes you laugh because it's so insane and unbelievable. But I called it normal. This was just another day-in-the-life of Tim Ryan, business mogul and living-large superstar.

Of course, it didn't last. All addicts understand the Law of Diminishing Returns: you can keep investing more in your drinking or drug use, but the pleasure you get back shrinks all the while. You either keep investing more to get any level of pleasure, or you change the game.

Life changed the game for me. Within a couple of years, I buried that business, got my heart broken, packed up from New York, and returned to Chicago with my tail between my legs.

I wanted to sober up, I thought. But you know, looking back, I'm not sure that was true. What I really wanted was to stop experiencing shit from my own stupid actions. That was it. I wanted a shit-umbrella that I could pop open when crap started raining down on me.

Back in Crystal Lake, my parents took pity and let me move back in while I tried to get my shit together.

I saw an ad that said, "Double your income." Two times zero is still zero. But I needed to start rebuilding somewhere, so I picked up the phone and set up a meeting with the guy on the other end. Kenny invited me to his home.

I didn't wait long after ringing the doorbell. Kenny eagerly popped out wearing a suit and tie. Plastered with a big smile and tons of energy, he pumped my hand. I wondered if this guy was peddling drugs or a cult. Normal people weren't that happy or enthusiastic.

He led me into his beautiful basement office with a rich, expensive-looking mahogany desk and huge, black leather chair against the wall. Light from the ceiling-level windows streamed in from all sides. Taking in the whole room, I noticed a white board with "1994: $180,000" written in red ink.

"Hey, Kenny. Tell me about that." I pointed to the board. "What's going on there?"

"That's how much money I've made this year." Kenny looked for a reaction.

"Dude, it's the end of February." Awe and skepticism mixed into my tone.

"Exactly. That's what I've built." He grinned.

"What the hell do you do? You a contract killer or something?"

"Ha! No, I'm a headhunter." I'd never heard of a headhunter. I'm guessing the look on my face told Kenny I was picturing cannibals who dried heads in the back room, because he quickly qualified: "I'm a data processing recruiter. I get jobs for people in the data processing space."

Holy shit, I need to do that, I thought. *I don't know what it is, but to make six figures in a couple of months, I'd be willing to do just about anything.*

Kenny started interviewing me to see if I was the kind of person who could help him build the business and make him even more money. But instead of answering his first question, I saw a book on his desk called *A New Pair of Glasses*. I'd seen it before. It was a 12-step, recovery-based book.

"Are you sober?" I asked. It might seem like an odd question to ask in an interview, but I wanted to take control of the conversation. It's what I did in sales, and in this case, I was selling myself.

"Yeah, seven years," he said. "Why?"

"Well, I'm two years sober." I smiled at him. Selling myself required small truths wrapped around huge lies. I had been sober for less than two days, but those days felt like a couple of years.

"No shit?" His face lit up. "Well, you've yourself got a job."

Addicts lie. And for a while, they get away with it.

I did.

CHAPTER 10

LIVING LARGE

Kenny was a phenomenal teacher. He gave me a simple script: "Hi, my name is Tim Ryan. I'm a data processing recruiter. The reason for my call…"

In no time, he took me from clueless to competent in the recruiting business.

Back then, we worked with IBM mainframes and AS400s. I closed my first deal at my 30-day mark when I placed a database analyst at a big company. Our fee was $18,750.

"What do I make on this, Kenny?" I asked, accepting his high five.

"Tim, you just made your first 9 Gs!"

Shit, I can do this all day! I thought.

That was March. In August, I did five deals in one month, made about $30,000, and never looked back.

Let me clarify that. I never looked back to any other way of making money. But of course, I jumped right back into drinking and doing drugs.

Nothing changed.

Kenny eventually figured it out, too, but he didn't care. I was his best employee, and I was a recruiting machine. No way was he going to let me go. I made too much money for him to get all moralistic on my ass.

We worked with a lot of management consulting firms. In a year's time, we placed about 20 people in one company. I met a vice president at one of those companies named Randy. He ran his firm's interests in Boston while building business in the Chicago market.

Most addicts learn to hold a grudge like it's an Olympic torch. As a little time passed, Kenny started pissing me off. When you hold onto resentment, each new negative situation just piles on top of the last one until it tips you over.

When I sat in Porter's Oyster Bar drinking and doing cocaine, I was thrilled when Randy called to tell me that he was looking for a full time recruiter of his own. After Randy asked me a few questions, I knew that I had this job if I wanted it. Whatever Kenny had done to piss me off most recently was still on my mind, so I jumped ship immediately. Randy gave me a $45,000 base salary. I was 26 years old, working for a management consulting firm. Everyone there had a college degree, many had Master's, and some had Ph.D.s. I had barely passed high school.

I plugged in hard. I was the best recruiter they'd ever seen. Very quickly, I was hiring 20 people per month at a commission of $3,000 per head. I'm not great at math, but I could feel the wad of 20 grand in my pocket each month. Since he knew I was good for it, Randy gave me a $6,000 a month draw against commissions, plus a base salary. I was making a six-figure guaranteed income plus commission. I got a new Harley and Jeep. Life was good again.

More money meant more and better booze and drugs. With a few drinks and snorts in me, I was Superman. I owned this game, and everyone around me knew it.

Soon I got promoted to director of recruiting and had a couple of other recruiters working under me. I realized that for me to do what I did best, I needed to hire an admin to help. Our organization ran on employee referrals. Why hire some unknown person off the street when I could hire someone known, proven, and liked?

An employee gave me a resume of this gal, Shannon, who worked at a bank. I didn't like bankers, because I always bounced checks. Bankers didn't like me, and it pissed me off to even think about dealing with them. There's a saying: *bitterness* only *consumes the vessel that contains it*. How deep was my resentment towards banks and bankers? I would take my commission checks for 15 to 20 grand and go cash them at a currency exchange. *Fuck the banks.* I could get my money quicker at the exchange anyway, and I've yet to meet a drug dealer who takes a check or credit card. Besides, I thought I was cool walking around with 10 grand in my pocket.

I stopped reading Shannon's resume when I saw the word *bank.* I never called her. But a month later, I saw this attractive woman sitting at the front desk of our office. I scanned her figure, which fit perfectly in her peach suit.

"Hey peachy, how ya' doin'?"

"Good," she answered with a smile, sizing me up.

"Who are you?" I got to the point—my frankness mixed with drugs, alcohol, and general impatience.

"I'm Shannon, the new receptionist. Who are you?" Her sweet voice sounded sincere.

"I'm Tim Ryan, director of recruiting."

"Oh, you're the guy who didn't want to hire me." She almost seemed to be flirting.

"What are you talking about?" I tried to use charm to cover up anything I might have done to taint her view of me.

"I'm Wylie's sister-in-law," she said. "He gave you my resume last month?"

"Well, damn," I said. "Obviously, I made a BIG mistake." I hoped to come across as sincere and nice. "Let me make it up to you. I'll take you out for a drink next week." I figured I'd sweet talk my way out of her doghouse and butter her up with some good times.

Our office was off Cumberland Avenue right next to a restaurant. I interviewed most potential hires at the restaurant, because, hell, I could work, drink, and smoke cigarettes at the same time. I also wanted to see how much they drank, because I needed good quality hires. I had problems with alcohol and drugs, but my delusional thinking said that as long as I was making money, I was okay to drink. Hell, drinking was *good* for me. But other people? I didn't trust them to work for me and knock back a bottle.

Double-standard much? Yeah, all of the time. That's just another lovely trait of a diseased, addicted mind.

What I didn't admit to myself at the time was that drugs were woven through every job I had. For example, I helped a consultant move one day. Turns out, his cousin, Joe, was a big cocaine dealer. I loved money AND cocaine. So I started dealing cocaine with Joe on the side. *Why not?* I thought. As a user/dealer, I'd save money. At the time, I was using a quarter ounce (called an eight ball) of cocaine and functioning. I'd go home, go to bed at 3 a.m., and get up at 5:30. And I never missed a beat or a day at work.

At first.

No one can live like that for long without burning out. My weekends of partying started costing me Mondays. I was too fucked up to get out of bed and function after days of abuse. But it was fine with my boss and the company because, like always, I made sure that I was so damn good at what I did, they couldn't replace me.

One morning walking through the office, I stopped to see Shannon. "Hey, good-looking," I said with a smile. "How about tomorrow night you let me and Evan take you out for a drink after work?"

She agreed, and the next night the three of us had a drink and got to know each other socially. When Shannon finished her drink, she got up. "Well, I really appreciate it, boys, but I have to get going. I have a son at home, and he's going to need his mama to get him to bed." She went to the bathroom before driving home, while my partner, Evan, and I ordered another round. "I got her," Evan said, licking his lips and giving me a devilish smile.

"No, this one's in the bag, buddy," I set him straight. "She's mine." I stood up and waited for her to come out of the ladies' room. When I saw her smiling face, I leaned into her cheek and planted a kiss.

"You're my new girlfriend," I told her.

Confidence, drugs, and alcohol. Yeah, I had the whole package.

She laughed nervously. "Yeah, okay," she said, with a non-committal laugh. "I'd like to go out on another date with you. I mean, a real date."

After I helped her put on her coat, she turned, looked me square in the eyes, took a deep breath, and said, "I have one question to ask. Do you do drugs?"

"God, no, I don't do drugs!" I lied as natural as breathing. "Why would you ask that?"

"Well, I have a 3-year-old son, Nick. His deadbeat, drug-addicted dad abandoned him. I don't want anything to do with a drug addict."

I kept smiling, hoping she wasn't a mind reader. "Nooo," I said, "I don't do drugs."

Shannon drove back to Naperville that night, probably wondering if she'd just met a guy who was going to change the direction of her life.

For my part, I drove to Chicago to buy another quarter ounce of cocaine.

CHAPTER 11
THE SEARCH IS OVER

Shannon and I started dating. She stayed with me in my new townhouse while keeping her own place in Naperville.

Even though I was making more than six figures, it was Shannon who cashed in part of her 401k to put a down payment on a 1994 Ski Nautique that I wanted. I was too much of a big shot to spend my walking-around drug money to buy something I wanted. So I used her money.

Addicts use people. Instead of feeling shame, I felt good that I got my girlfriend to pay for this expensive new toy and all of the gear, despite my lucrative job. I justified this by telling myself that we spent much of our time with Nick on the boat. So they were getting something out of it too.

Life felt easy and good for a time.

About four months into our relationship, Shannon sat me down. "Tim, I'm pregnant." She didn't beat around the bush. She looked me in the eye, waiting for my reaction.

Wow, I didn't know what to think. It hadn't occurred to me that I could be a dad, but I figured, *why the hell not?* Shannon was something special, and I knew we could do it.

"Well, that's awesome!" I said. She sighed in relief, smiling and throwing her arms around the man she envisioned as her prince charming. We started planning our wedding.

I loved that Shannon could keep up with my adventurous spirit. We'd drink on the boat by day. At night, we'd hang out at Porter's Oyster Bar, which my buddy owned. We'd bring Nick, listen to music, and enjoy ourselves. It's like we already were a family. Adding another kid, well, that would be icing on the cake.

But the difference between Shannon and me is that she could nurse three or four beers all day long and then stop. Not me. I'd wake up hammering the bottle, and I kept it going all day long. On top of that, even though she didn't know it at the time, I spent my nights shooting just as much coke up my nose as I was pouring drinks down my throat.

After a day of drinking on the boat, I decided to stop in Carpentersville to buy some crack. I finished a beer and tossed the empty bottle out of my Jeep window. A Barrington cop was coming the other way. That was my first DUI.

When Shannon found out, she was pissed. But I told myself: *Hey, I make the money around here. I can do whatever the hell I want with it.*

Addicts find excuses and justifications for their behavior. Had I set an orphanage on fire, I'm sure I could have made my actions sound noble or, at least, acceptable.

I got cockier at work. This guy, Justin, some stuffed shirt with an MBA, got bumped up to manager. Right after Evan and I pulled off an amazing job fair, Justin said, "We have a problem here. I just found out you guys make more money than I do, and I'm the branch manager. I'm the big boss."

"Not my problem, amigo," I told him. "We're damn good at what we do." And apparently, I wasn't done talking, so I added a little something. "Now go fuck off."

Travis, the vice president, overheard me and jumped in. "Tim, what the hell? You can't tell Justin to fuck off." His voice left no wiggle room, but I didn't care.

"Fuck him and fuck this place. I quit. I'll go start my own search firm." And with that, I walked out the door.

Now I had no choice but to start my own firm. I went from making six figures a year to making nothing. I quickly learned the big difference between being a top salesman and running a business. While trying to get my own company off the ground, Shannon and I had to sell the townhouse and her home.

No amount of confidence, drugs, or booze can compensate for incompetence. My company never took off.

Finally, I put my tail between my legs and accepted a job at another consulting firm at a $40,000 base. Shannon was five months pregnant. We moved into a dumpy apartment in Naperville. The sewage backed up in the tub. Strips of paint peeled off on the walls. Piss-poor space heaters hummed in every room. We were so broke we decided to screw having any sort of big party and did a courthouse wedding instead.

But our honeymoon was top-notch. We stayed at Kohler Lodge, a beautiful five-star resort in Wisconsin. We couldn't afford it. Fortunately, we didn't have to. Our honeymoon started the same night as the Christmas party at Travis's firm. Travis feared I would attend and recruit everybody to come work for me. So he paid for our honeymoon.

Soon afterwards, my son, Max, was born.

Life went on. Thrilled to find a beautiful, three-bedroom townhouse in Naperville, we moved in.

Shortly after, Shannon found some cocaine I'd hidden in the garage. "What the hell is this?" she asked me, stone faced.

"Oh, it must be Chad's," I lied on demand, blaming it on my buddy. I had no problem throwing someone else under the bus if it saved my hide. "Cuz I've never seen that before."

People who love addicts want to believe their lies. It's easier than facing the brutal truth. As soon as Shannon spoke to Chad, she learned the truth. But our worlds were already too deeply intertwined for her to consider leaving.

By this time, I'd legally adopted Nick. Being adopted myself, it was easy and natural to love Nick just like I loved Max. Nick was five, Max was just over a year, and Shannon was pregnant with our third child, a son we'd name Tanner.

Did getting married and having a family slow down my drug use? Hell, no. I'd disappear for two days at a time—snorting cocaine or smoking crack in the projects—I didn't care. And I'd do it in my own house.

One afternoon, I went on a coke bender and passed out. When I woke up, I saw Max out of the corner of my eye, crawling into my home office. I stumbled off the couch, snatched him in my arms, and plopped him into the crib in his room.

Opening my office door and peering into the dim light, my heart pounded. Cocaine crystals laced the surface of the office floor like chunks of hail. *If Max had picked up one of those rocks of cocaine and eaten it, it would have killed him,* I thought. *I have to get back to meetings.*

I started back into a 12-step program. It felt like a matter of life and death.

This was 1997 going into 1998. As my head cleared, I wanted to start another executive search firm of my own. This time, I committed to making it work. I recruited a genius high school buddy of mine, Damon. Damon had a full academic scholarship but never went to college. I said, "Damon, I want to teach you this business, and when you think you're ready, we'll go start our own firm." Within three months, he knew the business like the back of his hand. We found an investor who ponied up $20,000, and we started The Edge Recruiting in downtown Chicago, leasing office space on State and Wabash. We selected that location based on the building; it was in the first high tech, T1 line wired building where all the dot coms were moving.

The first year, we did $1.4 million. We pulled in $3.8 million our second year. The third year, the market hiccupped, and we were out of business.

I plugged into recovery. I remained clean and sober for the longest time since my teen years. I made it about a year. Looking back, my life was busy, but it was less chaotic, too. We rented a beautiful house in downtown Naperville. My son Tanner was born. Shannon got pregnant again, and my daughter Abby was born. Our family seemed perfect. My business grew and thrived. Hell, I ran the Cub Scouts.

I got a sponsor, and for the first time, started to work the steps. Halfheartedly, but I was working them. I met a guy named Reggie, who started coming to meetings after he got arrested. He and his girlfriend had OD'd on heroin. They had a baby. The authorities told them to stay clean and attend meetings, or they'd lose their child.

All 12-step programs have something called service work, where you do good things for people as part of your ongoing recovery. So when Reggie asked me to take him to Chicago to help him move out of his apartment, I was happy to help. As we carried furniture, his roommate came out of the bedroom and said, "You guys want to do a bag of heroin?" I was a year clean and sober, but I still wasn't living recovery. I was just going through the motions.

Fuck, yeah, I thought. This was not my first experience with heroin. I'd shot up once in New York, and I overdosed. *Well, that's no fun*, I told myself. So I stuck with snorting cocaine.

I decided the reason I'd overdosed the last time was because I'd shot up. This time, I'd snort it. *Yeah, it's not the drug. It's how you take the drug, right?*

"Yeah, I'll try a bag," I said. Within minutes, I was snorting that China white heroin. As it flooded my system, it did something for me that I hadn't experienced before. I felt like I belonged. I felt...alive.

This is what I've been searching for my whole life.

Most heroin addicts can tell you the drug makes you chase it. It's seductive in a way you can't control, but its charm distracts you from a black hole you can't escape.

From that moment on, I wasn't just chasing heroin. I was chasing my own destiny, and my choices would determine the destination. If I'd made bad choices before, I was about to make ones that were far worse.

For the first time, I wasn't obsessed with cocaine and booze. My appetite for heroin overtook all other urges. Within two weeks, I was snorting two $20 bags a day; by the end, I was snorting more than $500 a day.

When the wheels started falling off the dot coms, we bailed out of our recruiting business while the getting was good. I returned to a previous boss.

As a first time drinker and drug user, I was no stranger to blackouts, periods of time that I completely lost. But heroin was unlike any other. Shortly after I started this new job, I threatened to kill the whole staff. I had no recollection of it, but I learned about my newly unfolding violent side in detail: *you fuck me, I'll kill you.* My learning disabilities, my brother's insults and fist fights—you name it, I guess had an excuse for my swelling rage. I hurt a lot of people with that newly unleashed darkness. I got fired.

Despite my rages, I thought I was functioning fine.

I started working close to our home in Naperville. Reggie scored heroin in the city, and he'd bring it to me in the suburbs where I'd use and sell it. Shannon knew nothing about this.

When Reggie moved to California, I ran out of drugs.

That's the first time I got really sick from dope. I puked up bile and shook violently with freezing chills, even in the 90 degree summer heat. Shannon searched online to see if she could determine what "bug" I'd picked up. While she was in the next room, I called Reggie's supplier, Raja, who worked directly with the drug dealer, a guy named Ray.

"Dude, he's dope sick," I heard Ray say in the background. I hadn't heard the term before.

Being a man of action in a state of misery, I asked, "What do I need to do?"

"Stay put. I'll bring you a few bags of dope." Raja did just that. And boom, I was fine.

Ray's street name was "Boss Maniac." He was the third highest ranking leader in the Maniac Latin Disciples, the second largest Latin street gang in Chicago. Ray was technically retired, but he'd been in the game for a long time and still took special customers. Very quickly, I bypassed Raja and started dealing directly with Ray. Ray was happy I was his customer, because my habit lined his pockets with cold cash.

Shannon still had no clue what I was up to. We were a normal, suburban family. I ran the Cub Scout den as assistant pack master. Our kids grew like everyone else's. I worked from home, re-growing my consulting firm again, to the point where I made a quarter of a million dollars a year.

From my home office, I heard Nick tell his mom in the next room, "God, Dad seems happy all the time."

But I wasn't.

CHAPTER 12
EVER DEEPER

Nick's words bothered me. *Was I happy?* I asked myself. I couldn't tell. I worked non-stop. And I spent time with the kids, didn't I? But to this day, I don't remember much of it, because what I snorted, smoked, or drank blurred the rest. I polluted myself inside and out, and I couldn't see what mattered most.

We built a beautiful, five-bedroom house in Oswego. I didn't want to move. I'd been going to a 12-step group in Naperville, which made me feel safer. Yeah, I know how it sounds, attending 12-step meetings while going through bag after bag of heroin. But it didn't seem inconsistent to me. Part of me still hoped that just by sitting in those rooms, recovery would somehow sink into my bones.

In August 2002, after moving to Oswego, I got my second DUI. I'd been at a wakeboard tournament in Ottawa, drunk. I was stopped, and I refused to blow. Since I'd already had a DUI in 1998, I lost my license for three years. I couldn't drive.

I went through cycles when I'd start looking at my life honestly. I'd see the destruction I caused in flashes. And I felt tremendous guilt and shame. I was destroying life for Shannon, who watched me lose job after job. And now she had to drive me around like her toddler.

But those negative emotions weren't enough to make me call it quits. In fact, to numb the guilt, I doubled-down and used harder to blur the devastation I was causing.

Heroin was harder to get back then. I'd been using for about a year. I took the train to Chicago every day, saying it was for work. Superman could fly. Spiderman could shoot webs out of his wrists. My superpower was lying.

One day, I'd had enough.

"Ray, I can't keep living like this," I told my drug dealer, who'd oddly become my friend. "I'm spending too much money on drugs. My wife deserves better."

"Then it's time to get on methadone," he suggested.

"What's that?" I asked.

"Go to the methadone clinic and find out."

I bought 10 bags of heroin from Ray and then stopped at a Starbucks where I snorted it all in the bathroom. Talk to an addict, and you'll know that it's the most common thing in the world to get high on the way to detox or rehab.

I walked right into the methadone clinic where I pissed in a cup. "Yeah, you're a heroin addict," they confirmed.

No shit.

I met with the doctor who hooked me up with methadone. "Is this stuff addictive?" I asked the tall guy in the white coat.

"No, not at all. You can get off it any time. It just takes away the cravings." He made it sound as benign as a bag of Skittles.

I got my first dose and went home. Now that I was off the hard stuff, I decided to come clean and face Shannon. "Shannon, sit down," I told her. "Listen. I'm a heroin addict." I came right out with it.

Her face went white. I could see her mind racing. I figured that, knowing Shannon, she was going into protective mode to see how she could help me.

"But don't worry, honey," I reassured. "I'm on this drug, methadone. It's going to get me off the junk and save my life."

I talked like a guy who'd swerved at the last minute to avoid wrecking the car and now wanted recognition for being a world-class driver. Little did I know of the crash that was coming.

I could see neurons firing as Shannon glued the pieces together. Now it fit—why I was sick for weeks on end. I wasn't dying of cancer or some weird bacterial infection. I was a junkie.

Shannon couldn't react. I thought she just loved me too much to beat me up about it—and make no doubts about it, she did give me her whole heart. But even if she'd wanted to kick me to the curb, she was stuck. We shared four kids, around two years apart. Our youngest, Abby, was a vivacious 3-year-old. Our oldest, Nick, was 11.

Shannon was trapped with few options but to stay hitched to a shooting star—and not the sparkling variety.

Every day I took a train to Chicago to get methadone. Eventually, I found a place in Downers Grove where Shannon could drive me. About four months in, on a cold April morning, as she blew up balloons for Max's eighth birthday party, I tripped on a Spiderman action figure on the floor and started screaming, "WHAT THE HELL IS GOING ON IN THIS HOUSE? WHY IS THERE ALWAYS SOMEONE'S SHIT ALL OVER THE FLOOR?!"

Shannon had had enough. "You have got to get off this drug. Methadone turns you into an angry monster."

I punched my own palm, picked up my phone, and dialed Ray again. "Dude, what do I do?" I asked my heroin mentor.

He paused, and I could hear his heavy breath over the whir of traffic near him. "Buddy, you've got to go back on heroin."

I hung up, holding my head in my hands and shaking. I sat like that when Shannon walked in. "Baby, he says I have to get back on heroin," I said, as if Ray were my doctor writing a script for antibiotics.

She left the room. I didn't know what to do at this point. I couldn't feel the pain I caused her, but I could see it.

Less than a minute later, Shannon returned with a wad of bills and thrust them at me. "Here's $400," she said, "Go!"

Happy fucking birthday, Max. Shame mixed with relief fueled me into the city.

I'd given Shannon a dream house and everything she ever wanted materially. But I'd also given her something else: the misery of loving a full-blown junkie.

She kept our dirty little secret close to her vest. It wasn't exactly dinner party conversation. "Yeah, Sally Sue, Tim had a great time at the Cub Scouts camp-out with your son. They caught a big perch. And by the way, he won't be joining us for the cookout tonight, because he's shitting himself on account of his heroin addiction. Oh, and could we borrow a few bucks? Tim lost his job again for telling his boss to fuck off while on a bender."

Behind the scenes, Shannon did everything she could to fix me, to get me off dope. She even found this place in the jungles of Thailand with Buddhist monks. She would have bought me a plane ticket to Thailand to camp out in a monastery, if it would kill my addiction.

In her research, she learned about a drug named Suboxone, another opiate that removes cravings. We took the train to Chicago, where I met a prescribing doctor in the Wrigley building. We paid him $500 cash a week for seven pills.

I used Suboxone, but not to get clean. I kept using heroin, but the Suboxone kept me from getting as dope sick when I missed a fix. My addiction was managing me, and it got more demanding by the week.

When I did black tar heroin, it took eight hours before I'd get severely dope sick. While on China white, I could go 24 hours. Being dope sick on heroin is like having the flu times 1,000. My body was overcome with shaking, restless legs, puking myself, shitting myself, hot flashes, and cold chills. I'd sit in the hot bathtub and tell the kids to bring me popsicles. I'd smoke weed to try to stop the vomiting. You might try heroin for the first time at a party and feel like you are a rock star, but when you quickly become an addict, you realize you'd have more dignity swimming in a sewer. Addicts lie. And heroin lies. It whispers sweet promises of a magical experience. The magic is that it converts good times into bad and leaves you with a sickness that lasts ten times longer than the high. It turns dreams into nightmares.

CHAPTER 13

BUSINESS IN INDIA

Usually after three days without heroin, I'd get over the peak of physical misery. Then I'd start all over again. I couldn't get off its incestuous roller coaster. It kept taking me around and around. It might pause to let people on or off, but I was sure as hell going around again, no matter who stayed with me.

And yet somehow, the consulting business still allowed me to make great money.

Suboxone worked for a while, but I was hardly attending meetings, which meant I was imploding. I was either high, sicker than a dog, or a ball of rage.

I still didn't have my license back, but we bought a car six months before my three year suspension would be over. During a family vacation in Michigan, I desperately needed a fix. The demands of heroin were getting higher, and the amount of time I could go between fixes was getting shorter.

I cut the vacation short, and we headed back. I justified driving to "give Shannon a break." But as I drove us back, the voice of the addiction inside my head kept shouting, "Hurry! Hurry! Hurry!"

I got pulled over in Blue Island for changing lanes without a turn signal. Nice. This was the first time I'd driven without a license, and I got ticketed for driving on revoked. *Shit luck?* I wondered. In hindsight, I think God was allowing me to "load the bases" for what the future had in store.

The judge tacked on two more years without driving privileges on top of the three years I'd previously been sentenced.

Screw it, I told myself. *Go fuck with somebody else. I'm not playing by your rules anymore.* The addict in me felt such rage and resentment against the system. *What a crock!* When had I ever played by the rules?

Two weeks later, I got pulled over in Chicago by Officer Fred. Where was I going? To Ray's house to buy heroin. I carried recovery literature with me for times like this. I told Officer Fred, "Oh man, sorry. I'm going on a 12-step call."

Officer Fred didn't buy a word of it. He said, "Man, I know what you're up to. You better get yourself some help, and you better quit driving, because they're going to put you in prison."

He wrote me two tickets: driving on a revoked license and blowing a red light.

"What do I do now?" I asked him, stuck there with a car but no license.

"Drive home," he said. "Carefully," he added. "And for God's sake, get help."

"Sure thing," I replied, lying again. I continued on my path to Ray's and bought heroin.

I did two weeks in Cook County Jail for the first revoke charge, then later I did another two weeks.

On Mother's Day weekend, I headed out to buy Shannon a roast at the butcher shop. Of course, the butcher happened to be right next door to Ray's house, where I needed to stop to buy more heroin. Well, maybe the butcher wasn't right next door. It might have been 50 miles away.

Anyway, I got pulled over again. This time they impounded the car.

Shannon took me to get the car the next day. I drove right out of the impound yard and headed straight to Ray's to buy more heroin.

Two months after that, I drove our van to Chicago to Ray's house for more heroin. A police car pulled up behind me, flashed its lights, and ran the siren.

The officer approached my car and motioned me to roll down my window. "Man, you look familiar," he said.

"Officer Fred, good to see you. You stopped me eight months ago," I said, wondering in the back of my head if there was even the slightest possibility that I could get out of this mess.

"Damn it, I told you to quit driving," he said, shaking his head. He took my identification and returned to his squad car. Officer Fred ran my record. I had a warrant out for a medical bill I hadn't paid 10 years earlier. Ironically, I didn't ignore the warrant to show up in court for that bill; I never received it, because it was sent to an old address. But of course, I had a bunch of other recent arrests and charges for him to find.

Walking back to my van, Officer Fred shook his head and said, "Tim, this is a felony, man. I gotta take you in." The medical bill didn't look good, but it was the fourth driving on revoked that was the nail in my coffin that day.

In court, I was given the option of six months in Cook County jail, where I'd serve every one of those days, or a year in state prison.

"Take the year," my lawyer said. "You'll do 61 days and be released. Just know that you'll have a felony on your record."

"What the hell do I care? Do you think I'm going to run for President? I'll take the year," I said.

As the day neared when I'd start serving my sentence, Shannon and I sat down with the kids. "We have some exciting news, kids," Shannon said, trying her best to look and sound upbeat. "Daddy's going to India on business."

Nick was 15, Max was 9, Tanner was 8, and Abby was 6. They actually cheered for me, because it sounded pretty exotic to have a dad working overseas. Then they clung to me, because they were going to miss me. If I'd noticed any of this, I would have cried like a baby. But my mind was elsewhere: scoring some dope before I left for "India."

Unemployed again before my grand trip to Asia, I cashed in my 401K and gave it to Shannon.

"Keep that money away from me," I told her. "That's to pay bills while I'm gone."

I started cutting back on heroin and took Suboxone so I wouldn't be as severely dope sick. But staying in Chicago the night before I began my sentence, I went right back to heroin.

Live now, pay later. That had become my mantra for everything.

The two months I spent in the Vienna Correctional Center in southern Illinois felt like a fucking eternity. I remember the first time I called home. It felt so good that I called again. Eventually, I called home five times a day.

Abby turned 7 while I was in "India." Max turned 10.

My sobs echoed through my cell all day. Without drugs in my system, my emotions had no protection. No lies I might wish to believe could make missing two of my kids' birthdays okay.

The word PRISON came up on the caller ID on Shannon's telephone. "Oh, look! Dad's calling from the Pri-SOHN (said in a made-up foreign accent) Hotel in India!" she told the kids.

My whole life was a lie. I could no longer believe myself, because the biggest whoppers I told were to myself. I was losing my wife, my kids, and my mind.

I will not surrender to this disease, I told myself. *When I get back home, I'm done with drugs and booze.*

Lies. All lies. Nothing changed. Good intentions mean shit with no plan and no Higher Power to walk with me.

The reunion with my family when I got out was like Christmas. We hugged, I told stories about "my travels," and the kids went to bed happy that their world-traveling father was home.

With the kids asleep, Shannon sat me down. "Tim, I got a full ride scholarship to nursing school. I was number one out of 10,000 applicants. I won a Dunham Scholarship." I could hear her pride and determination.

"Shannon, look, you don't need to work. I make plenty of money."

What utter bullshit. I'd just gotten out of prison. I was unemployed. And even when I made good money, I spent it on smack and legal bills.

She looked at me squarely, her eyes flashing. Her lips moved nervously, as she formed her words. My mind flashed back to Dad telling me he was done with my bullshit, when I was in rehab.

"Tim." Shannon calling my name pulled me back to the present. "The way you're living, you're going to end up in one of two places," she said. *"You're going to end up dead, or you'll be back in prison."*

She made it clear that neither option would work for her. "We've got four kids, and I can't rely on you."

Her words hit me like a dump truck.

True, I'd overdosed a few times. And I'd been arrested a few times. And I didn't have the best track record for keeping steady employment. She made some good points there.

But there was no way in hell I was going back to prison. That was not an option in my book.

Two weeks out of incarceration, I started another executive search firm. I had a good client out of the gate and made around $400,000 that year.

I went to visit Ray. I'd heard that his wife had died from a drug overdose. I wanted to offer my support, and I wanted to see his wife Phoebe's grave.

And you know what? I could have passed a polygraph test on every one of those lies I told myself as I drove to Ray's house. These people weren't my true friends; they were my drug dealers, people who helped keep me in the chains of my addiction. I was the only white person allowed in this family's home, and it wasn't because they liked me. I knew Ray's extended family, including all four of his daughters. One of them told me once, "Tim, nobody talks to my dad the way you do. If you had done this in the gang, you'd be dead."

I was still alive, because you don't kill the goose laying the golden eggs.

Ray pulled out 10 syringes of dope, already made up, and shook them at me, "Do you want one?"

Of course I did. I got right back on the horse.

One afternoon, I walked into the basement of my home in Oswego and found Nick, 16, with two girls smoking a joint. When the girls saw me, they freaked out and tried to hide their stash and look sober. Nick laughed at them. "What, you don't smoke pot with your dad?"

I thought I was the coolest dad in the world. In hindsight, I was a piece of shit. I was not a father to my son. I was a friend—and not a good one at that.

As my addictions grew, Nick started getting in and out of trouble. But I hardly noticed. My world revolved around me.

One December night, feeling guilty for all of my selfishness, I decided to orchestrate the Christmas of all Christmases. I bought Shannon diamonds and Coach purses. I got the kids nice clothes, music, and every toy they wanted. I was Super Dad and Husband.

For about three hours.

But the reverie of the gifts couldn't last past my next craving. At about 10 a.m. Christmas morning, I called a cab for Chicago. I was getting dope sick.

My memories of that Christmas aren't about all the nice things I bought everyone else. They are about riding in a puke-stinking cab to the shitty side of the city so I could get my fix. The kick in the ass is that the more drugs I used, the more I listened to the lies of addiction that told me, "*We're fine. We're still having fun together, aren't we?*"

The insanity of my disease had me spinning so fast that everything around me blurred.

My lies expanded to include Shannon's life. Just as I told myself that I was still okay, I think Shannon eventually told herself that my heroin addiction was a natural part of life. And why not? I cleaned house. I worked hard and made money when I wasn't screwing things up at work. Shannon was done fighting with me. She'd given up and was focusing on nursing school and being a good mom. She couldn't fix me, so she checked out.

Any person outside of my life would see a well-off scout leader living with his family in a lovely home. They'd see my beautiful wife and fantastic kids. What they couldn't see was the heroin in my veins, and the addiction consuming me from the inside out.

But you can't hide the truth forever.

CHAPTER 14
A WHITE CHRISTMAS

The winter of 2010 hit us hard. It was December 16, and the next day Shannon was having all the students from nursing school over for a big party to celebrate their upcoming graduation. She was upstairs taking a shower. I'd been drinking. I planted on the couch and pondered my next move.

It was freezing outside, and the wind was howling like it does only in the Midwest. My wonderful, beautiful wife was upstairs naked in the shower.

Why don't I join her in the shower and make love to her?

That's what a normal person might think. That's what I wished I'd been thinking. But at the time, that thought never even crossed my mind.

Instead, I patted down Shannon's coat until I found where she'd hidden the money for her party. I grabbed the wad of cash and stuffed it into my jeans' pocket.

The keys jingled in my hand, as I pulled my coat from the closet. I didn't have much time now. I heard Shannon's feet pounding down the stairs. I looked back at her over my shoulder, as I opened the door leading to the garage. Her hair was still wet, and the towel was barely covering her.

"Tim, I know what you're doing. Please turn around!" At first she sounded angry. When her words didn't change my course, she tried something else. Her voice raised an octave. "Tim, I love you! We'll get help! Please don't do this, please." She was sobbing, and I couldn't tell where her tears left off and her wet body began.

When you love an addict, you may think you've given up on that person, but there is always a way to be hurt again. That's what I was doing to Shannon.

This wasn't about Shannon. It was about me. Once my switch was on, there was no stopping it. I wanted heroin. No, screw that. I *needed* heroin. And I couldn't hear my wife or kids clearly. All I could hear was the lie of the addiction screaming, *"It's you and me, kid! Let's go! Everything will be fine. But we have to hurry…"*

Ray was dead. He committed suicide. He couldn't handle life without his wife. So I had started buying from his sister-in-law, Brenda, and her husband, Larry. I pulled up to their house and knocked on the door. Brenda invited me in, went into the back room, and brought me a few bags of heroin.

"Be careful, Tim," she said, sounding oddly like my mother. "We just got a new batch, and this stuff is strong."

I drove away cautiously, as if I needed to protect this hot stash of potent drugs in the car—all while my precious family sat at home, needing me.

I pulled over into the parking lot of McDonald's on Grand and North Avenue. *I'll just shoot up a little bit and see how heavy it really is*, I thought.

I filled the needle, tied off my arm, and injected my vein through my scarred skin. I slid it out smoothly, cleaning off my syringe and spoon and sticking it behind the driver's seat. I'd gotten really good at injecting myself, as if that was something to be proud of. *That's funny*, my head started to float away. *Shannon is going to be a nurse, but I'm the expert with needles.*

My thoughts kept drifting for a minute as I sat in the car. *Well, shit*, I thought. *I'm not dead.*

So I started driving. Within what felt like seconds, a flash of different colored lights hit me, like the stars I'd seen when my brother had slapped me in the head as a kid.

Next thing I knew, I wasn't driving anymore. I had no idea how much time had passed. I might have been there a whole day, for all I knew. Time had swallowed itself, just as blackness kept swallowing up the lights.

Some guy ran up to my car. "Hey, man. I've got a tow truck. I'm going to help you out," he said. I didn't know him from Adam, but he seemed trustworthy. I was in no position to argue.

I pulled the keys from the ignition and placed them in his gloved hand.

"I'm going to jail. Tow my car so the police don't get it," I instructed him. Even though I didn't know what had happened, I knew if I got caught behind the wheel, I'd be going away for a long time.

Then my lights went out.

When I regained consciousness, I was on a gurney being wheeled into West Suburban Hospital. *I don't have my glasses on, and I can't see a damned thing. Why is this nurse asking me questions?* My thoughts were entirely self-absorbed. I had to get out of this situation, and I'd do anything for a break to freedom.

"My name is Tim Ryan," I mustered, trying to insert some charm despite my circumstances.

"Where are you from?" the sweet voice asked. She sounded like Shannon.

"Naperville. Crystal Lake," I said.

"Hold on. Are you Tim Ryan the water skier?" She sounded too perky for my mood.

"Yeah, that's me," I said, trying to get a look at this woman who apparently knew who I was. All I could see were bright lights and blonde hair.

"I went to high school with you!" She seemed momentarily starstruck in a small town way, before remembering what lie in front of her. "Do you know you're in a lot of trouble?" she asked in a lowered tone.

Ya think? I thought.

"You need to get your shit together," she said as she adjusted the IV in my arm. What she said next turned my world upside down and sent it flying end over end. Time slowed, and her words sounded like they came through spinning fan blades. "*I. Think. You. Killed. Some. People.*"

Oh. My. God. I squeezed my eyes together tightly, trying to stop what I'd just heard.

Cops started swarming around my bed like wasps around an open soda can. I wasn't handcuffed yet.

One cop kept yelling in my face, "You motherfucker. You killed two people, you junkie piece of shit. You fuckin' just killed two people."

I kept my eyes closed, but I couldn't stop the accusations. *What the hell? I can't remember a damned thing*, I thought. Everything went blurry again and kept zooming in and out of focus.

"Let's get blood and urine," I heard a nurse say. I opened my eyes, and I saw a cop turning the corner. Finally, there wasn't an officer in sight. I dove off the gurney, somehow got to my feet, and started to run down the shiny hallway.

Apparently, my sight wasn't reliable. Five cops swarmed me instantly. Dragging me back to the bed, they shackled me to its frame.

"You ain't goin' nowhere," one of them taunted. His eyes twitched. He was visibly angry, and it dawned on me that he'd probably kill me if he thought he could get away with it.

How do I get out of this mess?

"You've got to check me out of here," I said. "I don't have any insurance." Which was true. *As if that was my biggest problem.* Even though I made great money through the years, I never bothered with insurance. When you overdose or have a heart attack because of drugs, they take you to the ER. Those bills aren't small. And they don't go away, either. "I want to go. Just take me to jail." I sounded like a martyr.

"Sure thing, buddy!" they said. This is what they were waiting to hear. It would save them time. They got me up, and I signed myself out.

I didn't really give a crap about the insurance. I was already in protection mode. I thought: *They got no blood or urine. I'll beat this bitch.*

I'd just been told that I'd killed two people, but what was I worried about? Saving my own ass.

At the station, an officer booked me and started taking my fingerprints.

"Kid, you okay?" he asked in what sounded like a genuine tone. "No, I'm pretty fucked up right now," I admitted.

"Hey, look at me," he said, waiting for my eyes to find his. "You didn't kill anyone," he said.

I shook my head. Instead of relief, my first emotion was deep anger. I'd been lied to. I wanted to yell at someone, but I was too messed up to react.

"My partner is really pissed off at you," the booking officer continued. "He's sick of junkies, and a lot of them do end up killing people. That's why he told you that for the past four or five hours." Then he added, "You did put four people in the hospital, one of them a 9-month-old baby."

I thought of Abby, Max, Ryan, and Nick—my babies.

"How are they—the people in the car?" I mustered.

"I think they're all going to be okay." Something about his eyes showed compassion, even after all I'd done. I didn't deserve it. I looked away.

Getting processed through Cook County Jail had become routine to me at this point. I laid in my rack. The guy in the bunk next to me started yammering.

"Man, are you okay?" He seemed hard up for conversation—or maybe something that resembled friendship.

"Dude, I'm going to prison again." I told myself this would never happen again. Jail is something you can shake off and go home from. Prison is another beast. Prison becomes your life. It ends up soaking into your bones, like a bad smell you can't get out of your nostrils. You never come back fully from prison.

"Well, what happened?" He didn't ask what I did. He asked me what *had happened*, as if I was the victim.

I responded with something, but I have no idea if it made sense.

"Man, when's the last time you ate?" he asked. The guy then went into his box and pulled out this big chocolate donut. "Here, man. Why don't you eat this?"

"I ain't got nothing to trade." I shrugged my shoulders.

"No. Listen, I'm a heroin addict too, and I know you need some food. I don't want anything." He gave me the donut.

Right there, that donut was a little bit of happiness.

The next morning, I called Shannon. And she let me have it. "Tim, you ruined my party. I had to cancel. I had 40 people who'd already had their hair done and made dishes to bring, and

I couldn't have a single one of them over. I had to make up some lame excuse about our plumbing being out. And where the hell is the van? The police don't know where our vehicle is."

I tried to piece things together in my head so she could get me out. She must have read my thoughts. "I'm not getting you out." *But it's Christmastime*, I thought. Again she read my mind. "You should have thought about that before you shot yourself up and lost our car." Shannon hung up on me.

I called my parents. "Tim, honey, we're not bailing you out," my mom said. She was nice about it, but she was trying her darndest to be firm with me. *She's pulling that Al-Anon shit*, I figured.

Dad got on the line, and he wasn't as sweet. "You're done. You made your bed. You lie in it." Dad had finally mastered tough love.

December 20th came. I called Shannon again, hoping she'd simmer down and change her mind. "I checked the voicemail on your cell phone." She was quiet for what felt like a minute, but it must have been a few seconds. *Okay*, I thought, waiting for whatever discovery came out of her mouth next. I had no idea what she'd say next. It could go either way. I could be in the dog house, or I could be redeemed a little bit. "I found the van."

"What are you talking about?" This still could be good or bad news, depending on her next words.

"When you overdosed, the guy who came up to the car was a tow truck driver, and you gave him the keys. Then you left. He towed the van. The police never got it. It's getting fixed, because the airbags went off."

I didn't know this at the time, but we had $2,000 worth of Christmas presents for our kids in the back of that van. That's where Shannon had hidden them. She wasn't calling me to tell me she was springing me out of jail. She was calling to tell me that the kids were going to have a good Christmas despite their deadbeat dad overdosing, wrecking their only vehicle, nearly killing four people, and getting arrested.

That's nice, I thought to myself. *But how does that help me? Me, me, me.*

I had to get out of there. I knew my mom was the weakest link, so I manipulated her hard. She put up bail money on December 23rd. Shannon sat at Cook County Jail for 10 hours waiting for me. I finally got released at 2 a.m., and it was freezing. I only had on a tee shirt and jeans. She drove me home.

"I'm going to bed." Her voice was stern but soft. She didn't know what to do with me at this point.

"Shannon, did they give you my coat? I think I left my glasses in the pocket," I asked her before she climbed the stairs.

"It was in the van. I hung it up in the closet. I put your glasses on your desk." I gave her a kiss good night and thanked her, and she went up to bed.

As soon as she disappeared around the corner upstairs, I nearly ran to the closet. Then I grabbed my coat and opened up the zipper of my pocket. All my heroin was still there.

I expertly tied off my arm and immediately shot up.

Merry fuckin' Christmas to me, I said to myself as my eyes rolled up into my head.

CHAPTER 15
OAK TREES AND LITTLE ACORNS

After Christmas, I got a job with a high-end recruiting firm in Chicago. This opportunity was a godsend.

But my legal woes racked up. I thought the police hadn't gotten to the van, but they had. The tow truck driver hadn't towed my van until the police had searched it. Turns out, the police were there the whole time. Apparently, they pulled my coat off me to put me on the stretcher, and then they threw my coat back into the van, not thinking it relevant to their case against me. I found this out while I was fighting the case. But what they found in the van was enough: the spoon and syringe I put behind the passenger seat.

They charged me with my third DUI and my fifth driving on revoked. The syringe behind the passenger seat had 1/10 of 1 percent of 1 gram of heroin, so they added a charge of drug possession. If they'd checked my coat, I would have gotten another 10 years for drug trafficking.

I now see this as another God moment, perhaps one more chance to see what I'd do with my life in the coming years.

I waited for my sentencing. And I started counting up the ways I'd beat this, just like I'd beaten the odds after each overdose and arrest, just like I'd kept my marriage intact, just like I'd managed to keep getting jobs making obscene amounts of money.

They didn't get blood or urine at the West Suburban Hospital. I'll beat this shit. I know I will.

But another voice inside of me was asking, *how am I going to beat this*? So with the money from my new job, I interviewed two lawyers from high-end law firms in Chicago, and I selected Rob Sullivan. He was a gun. It ultimately cost me more than 30 grand, and I'd go to court 21 times.

Meanwhile, in the first three weeks of my job at the big firm, I popped five deals. They thought I was God. The company made a ton of money because of my work.

I met a guy named Devon through skydiving. He was from London, and he came to America to work in the technology space. He'd had a rough life, and he loved to party. So we quickly became partners in crime. Heroin, coke, booze—all in a day's work.

So, again, nothing changed. God gives me another chance, and I jump out of airplanes with enough drugs in my system to drop a horse.

A normal person would start to tally up all of the negative consequences that had drugs or alcohol as their cause. But I was far from normal.

I didn't dare drive to court. It wasn't a matter of once bitten, twice shy. I was five times bitten. Whenever I had to make a court appearance, I'd take the train to Chicago, hop on a bus over to 26th and California for my hearing, and then hop another bus to work. Oh, and of course I always made time for a heroin buy before leaving the city for the day.

My boys were all teenagers at the time, and Abby wasn't far behind. I had no secrets with my kids at this point. I would have liked to keep some things in the dark, but I'd screwed up too many times in too many public ways. My kids knew I was a heroin addict. They knew what was up. There was no more "Pri-SOHN Hotel." They came to terms with having a junkie-dad living at home for the time being.

Shannon was working at Dreyer Medical Clinic, trying to hold things together. About three months after my case began, dope sickness hit me like a brick one day. I got into a hot bath and felt like death. I didn't even notice the door opening. Nick walked into the bathroom without a sound.

"What's wrong, pops?" I opened my eyes and saw him standing in front of what looked like a blinding light.

"What do you think?" I said with sarcasm. "I'm dope sick."

He looked at me with a knowing smile. "Not anymore, Dad. Today's your lucky day." He left the room and returned, dropping two bags of heroin on the cold bathroom counter.

What is an addict? An addict is someone with a one-track, polluted mind. At that moment, I didn't think, *oh my God, my son just brought me heroin. What is wrong with this kid? How did he get caught up in this shit!?*

Instead, I told myself, *in two minutes, I'm not going to be sick anymore.* I got out of the tub, did those two bags of heroin, and walked into Nick's room. With my drug coursing through my veins again, I could think straight enough to be a "parent."

"What the fuck are you doing, Nick?"

"Don't worry, Dad. I'm just selling a little bit." He smiled like I should be proud.

"Nick, this isn't selling weed. Shut this shit down immediately." My voice vibrated through my body, while the heroin pulsed through my veins, begging me to slow down this conversation.

With eyes locked on me, he smiled. His next words vibrated far more strongly than my drug: "Well, Dad, you're a *successful drug addict.*"

My blood seemed to drain out onto the floor. I might not look like the model of a perfect dad, and I had no clue how to break the chains to my drug, but I still didn't want my actions to affect anyone—least of which my own son. "Why would you say that?" I really didn't want an answer.

"Look at us." He gestured around with his hands. "We've got a nice house. You've had an office in the Wrigley building. You make insane money."

I left his room, because I could say nothing. I wanted to put it behind me, as much as I wanted it to stop. But for that moment, I just wanted to sleep.

Addictions don't just stop on their own. They only get stronger and more convoluted. My grandiose mind could easily forget about any shame, as I pulled others into the drain of my life on heroin.

Three months later, Nick and I were snorting heroin together. The walls were caving in on me—but not just me.

Some days, my addiction seemed like it was under control, but it never was. It was just hiding out behind the next DUI or overdose or outburst, like a predator in the shadows, waiting to grab me by the wrists again, wring them into submission, and take me to places I didn't control.

I was drinking at work all the time. My boss and I went out at 11 a.m. to have a few drinks over lunch at a new bar/restaurant next door called South Branch. I had 10 vodkas and a bunch of shots. We went back to the office, and I remember nothing after that. I blacked out.

Later, my boss told me what I did. There were about 10 of us in the office that day. One was this lady who sat next to me, someone I never liked.

"Suck my dick," I told her, slurring. When she didn't react, I began stripping my clothes off. I dragged my junk out and said, "Here, why don't you suck on this?" Still not satisfied, I climbed onto the desk and started dancing in the buff.

Does that sound like something normal people do? A friend of mine, Scott, told me that when he started wondering if he had a drinking problem, he talked to a neighbor who he knew attended recovery meetings.

"Hey, you're an alcoholic, right? Do you think I'm an alcoholic?" Scott asked his neighbor.

"Scott, you're the only one who can answer that question. But I will say that you're the only person who has ever taken a leak on my front porch in broad daylight," his neighbor told him.

"Really," Scott answered, not believing what he heard.

"Twice," his neighbor added. Shortly after being confronted with the facts that he had blackouts, Scott entered recovery and never left.

Not me. I was hard core. And I knew that I wasn't normal. But I didn't want to be normal, not yet anyway. Sober, I was sharp enough to remember any name and face, and what that person had for breakfast. Impaired, I was out of control, and I was left piecing together memories from snippets of things other people told me.

I left work. But I wasn't done drinking. My buddy, Devon, and I went out to dinner and drank some more. Finally, I somehow made it home to sleep it off.

Once again, my problems weren't gone in the morning. They were worse. The ringing phone woke me up.

"Tim, my God." I recognized the voice on the line as the president of the company.

I had no idea what had happened, but I knew it must be bad. So I kicked into *cover your ass* mode. "I'm so sorry; it won't happen again." I used this line a lot.

"Tim, you're finished here. I'm going to get some lawsuits from this one. You're a great recruiter, but you're out of control."

A normal person would think, *How will I pay the mortgage? How will I take care of my family?*

But I was far from normal. I wondered, *What am I going to do for drug money?*

I'd been in business for myself so many times that I knew I could do it again to make some quick cash. I started making drug deals again to tide me over until the next job. A big festival called Summerfest was coming on at Skydive Chicago.

I'll just get a couple ounces of cocaine and sell it, I told myself. *People will be in from all over the world.*

I met Nigel from Australia. He was there for two weeks, and we did cocaine every day. He was a good customer who bought every bit of drugs I had with me, and he let me snort alongside him. He extended his visa and rented a trailer. In a matter of three months, we went through about 18 to 20 ounces of cocaine. At one point, Nigel and I sat up for 10 days straight snorting cocaine. I snorted right through my birthday, and I never so much as called home.

Shannon called a couple of days later. "Your kids miss you. When are you coming home?" She didn't say, "I miss you."

"Another day, another day…" I hung up. Nothing broke through to me. I was riding this horse hard, and I wasn't ready to stop.

"Hey, mate, we need some landing gear to come down from this cloud," Nigel said. So of course I went out for heroin.

As I sat in his trailer, feeling the heroin course through my veins again, I got another phone call. It was a consulting firm in Florida that wanted to interview me for a role in their new Chicago office. I went home, showered, shaved, changed, and hopped on a plane to Florida. I got the job and flew back. I partied through Sunday with Nigel doing cocaine; my new job started Monday.

I had the Midas touch. Everything I touched turned to gold. Even when I had a setback, I'd end up falling forward. I was bulletproof!

That's what the addiction told me. But it wasn't true.

When I showed up to work on Monday, I was fired when I walked through the door. I failed the drug test.

"What are you doing home?" Shannon asked, surprised to see my face when I'd just left house a couple of hours earlier.

"Oh my God, Shannon. They just shut down the Chicago office." Shannon looked at me, not sure what to believe.

Everything out of my mouth was a lie.

More jobs came and went. The pressure of court and life compressed me even more. Nick and I started doing drug runs together. I was unable to parent in any real way, and my head was a mess, so why not? At least we'd get to spend time together, I thought. Abe Sanders, one of Nick's best friends—and their buddy, Isaac—drove me to Chicago to get heroin. As we were driving back, I said, "Hey, do you guys want a bag for your trouble?"

"No, sir," Isaac's voice piped up quickly. I don't know if he was too shy to say yes to the father of one of his best friends, or if he just knew better, but that decision may have saved his life.

"I'll take one," said Abe. Abe practically lived at our house, since he was Nick's best friend. He was a couple of years older than Nick, and they'd already been smoking weed and partying together for years. But that was his first time doing heroin. Soon thereafter, he became a heroin addict.

The best way not to notice how fucked up you've become is to surround yourself with other people who are just as fucked up as you are. Camouflage works in any setting, not just the jungle.

CHAPTER 16
GOD, ARE YOU UP THERE?

I could run, but I couldn't hide. By October 30 of 2012, I'd run out of time for my court appearance. It was time to stand before the judge for sentencing.

As I said, presiding over my case was Judge Willis, a distinguished, gray-haired gentleman. My lawyer told me he was a Sox fan and a fair man. I didn't want fair; I wanted forgiving. I wanted a push-over.

"Tim Ryan, please rise," the bailiff called out at last.

My stomach tightened. My legs didn't want to support my weight as I slowly stood upright. This was the moment I'd been dreading. The heroin in my system made me numb, but not numb enough to block out what was about to happen.

"Fuck!" I muttered in disbelief that I found myself stuck between freedom and imprisonment. "Fuck."

My lawyer approached the bench, and I heard Judge Willis muttering something like, "10-12, 10-12."

I gathered from those words that Judge Willis wanted to give me 12 years. I looked at my lawyer with a shrug in need of an answer. He mouthed, "Hold on, hold on."

My lawyer and the judge continued talking, and then I heard the judge say, "3-3-1."

My lawyer walked back from the bench and stood next to me. I searched his face for some sort of answer, but at that same moment the judge announced his sentence:

"Seven years." "Seven years."

Judge Willis dropped the gavel along with my hopes of a cake-walk sentence.

"What?" I asked my lawyer. "What is 3-3-1? Am I going away for seven years?"

"No, listen. You got seven years total for all charges. You got three years, three years, and one year. With good behavior, you'll be out in a year and a half."

Eighteen months was a helluva lot better than the 7, 10, or 12 years that I could have gotten.

Immediately, the bailiff took me into the back where a Corrections Officer walked me to a holding cell. "Hey look, man, I need my coat," I told the CO. I had learned a thing or two since my accident about where to hide my stash.

"No, you don't need your coat," he replied.

"It's cold in those bullpens. Plus, it's got my wallet and cell phone, and I need to give those to my lawyer." The CO ignored me.

My lawyer, Rob, jumped in, knowing the CO wouldn't protest too much. Rob grabbed my coat and handed it to me. I gave him my wallet and cell phone, saying, "Mail those to Shannon."

The CO looked at me, as a light bulb went off in his head. "You're a heroin addict!" he said, grabbing my coat and pulling out my coat sleeve, slowly turning it inside out while looking at it carefully. "I bet you've got some needles hidden in here."

My heart pounded.

I looked him straight in the face and said, "Man, I've got a wife and four kids. Do you think I'd be stupid enough to bring drugs into a penal institution?"

The CO got a blank face and paused, letting the jacket go like a catch and release trout. "Yeah, I guess you're right."

Apparently, the CO had never been an addict, because addicts don't think. The addiction does all of the thinking for the person whose body it possesses.

Finally, the coat was back in my hands. Someone walked me out of the room and down a non-descript hall. As soon as they left me in a holding cell, I reached for my stash. My hands shook so badly that the bags of heroin started slipping through my fingers and onto the ground.

I knew cameras were all over, but I didn't care. I was going to prison anyway. I scrambled and scraped the rest of the bags out of my coat, ripped open a bag, and started snorting to get relief. The old familiar feeling was back, and I could relax for a bit. I tucked the rest back in my jacket for later.

Eventually, I got processed through Cook County Jail. I knew I had to go through the metal detector machine. I was sweating like crazy. I had more than fifty bags of heroin wrapped tightly in tin foil. I kept transferring the tiny packages from my shirt to my sock to my shoe, hoping they wouldn't get noticed. *I'll just cram it all in my sock and be done with it.* I tried to look confident walking through the machine, but I was shaking like a leaf. I don't know how I got through that machine without someone finding that bulge in my filthy sock, but I did.

Later, I'd learn that with the amount of heroin I was carrying, I would have added another 15 to 45 years to my sentence—even on a first offense—for carrying drugs into a penal institution. I had no idea of the risks I was taking that day; God, again, was giving me a chance.

But even if I'd known about the risk, it wouldn't have mattered. *I needed my drug*—or so I thought.

I don't remember much about Cook County Jail. I was so depressed at the thought of going to prison, I snorted all of my heroin within 24 hours. If it killed me, fine. At least I'd be out of the shit. I sat in holding for three days. The stench of the place made me want to die.

I couldn't wait to get on a bus to Stateville in Joliet, where I'd have some communication with the outside world. From there, I'd learn my prison assignment.

As I lay there in county jail, Shannon's words to me came back in the dark: *You're going to end up in prison or dead.* I needed Sheridan Correctional Institute, because in my research, I'd learned that they offered recovery services. Suddenly, my life seemed to depend on going to Sheridan.

I was awoken at 3 a.m. by some guys who were probably no happier to be shaken from sleep and immediately assaulted by the cold, stale jailhouse than I was. "Pack up; you're going to prison." Somehow this felt like a relief to be going somewhere and getting out of this stench. I caught myself in my thoughts: *How unmanageable has my life become that I'm happy to hear I'm off to prison?*

Outside, seven buses were running with exhaust plumes hanging off their backsides. A bunch of police cars hovered nearby to escort them.

The ride was quiet. Some prison regulars slept soundly on the bus; I sat with my eyes locked low in front of me, avoiding eye contact in the event anyone happened to look my way.

I never joined the military, but I'd seen movies about the boot camp experience where recruits were stripped of their individual identities. Of course, military recruits are heroes for their willingness to serve our country. We weren't heroes; we were criminals. Heroes help others; criminals help themselves until they get caught.

Indeed, they immediately stripped us of our identities. We were forced to line up. They took all of our possessions and ordered us to put on jumpsuits. They drew blood. They looked in our mouths. They had us bend over while they checked our nether regions for contraband. They had us talk to a shrink to determine just how crazy we were.

I had one objective: get to detox. My body had already started revolting on me, and dope-sickness was eating me from the inside out. When I finally got in front of the doctor, I told him, *"I'm a drug addict, and I need to go to Sheridan to detox."*

I knew that Sheridan was a long shot. There were 28 prisons they could send me to. I knew that Sheridan had detox and active recovery programs, so Sheridan was the hope I held onto.

Looking at my rap sheet and then at my strung out body, he nodded in a non-committal way. "If anyone needs Sheridan, you do."

A glimmer of hope. But until I got official word, it was like I stood in front of a firing squad with a blindfold on. The only part of that thought I liked was having a cigarette, but there was no cigarette on this firing line.

Funny. When I was free on the outside, my only obsession was scoring drugs. Now that I was an insider, my new obsession became finding a path to get clean. This new desire was a silent recognition for the very first time that I was powerless over drugs and alcohol—that my life had become unmanageable.

At the Northern Illinois Receiving Center, they put holding cell inmates in one of three wings called houses. Each house held about 10 cells. Once that door slammed, I was in it 24/7. I'd stay in that cell until they figured out what prison to send me to. It could be a week, it could be a month, or it could be three months. I'd never know until they told me. And, like a casino, I never knew what time of day or night it was. I had no windows to the outside world. The sky didn't exist. This dark world lacked song birds, fresh air, smiles, or human kindness.

Reality set in. On top of that, I began to get profusely sick. I vomited for days on end, and I was so weak, I couldn't direct the spray. Instead of bowing over the toilet, the bile pooled in the corners of my mouth and spilled down the front of my shirt. I shit all over myself. When I wasn't burning up, I was freezing. This lasted for two weeks.

Ah, the glamour of heroin.

As the sickness began to pass, I took more notice of my surroundings and my roommate—a guy from Rock Falls, Illinois. He slept 20 hours a day. I was jealous. Like me, he was in prison for an addiction—in his case, alcohol. He was a former Marine sniper with 38 confirmed kills. When he awoke, we'd talk a lot, and I assessed him to be a good guy. He told me what landed him in prison. He'd been at a Hooters when he saw a beautiful Corvette parked out front. Drunk off his ass, he stole the car out of the parking lot and parked it behind the building as a joke.

The guy who owned the car, the son of a police detective, didn't find humor in that prank. My cellie got charged with grand theft auto and sentenced to eight years in prison.

I'd never been away from actively using drugs for so long that I struggled to wake up or go to sleep. As the heroin exited my body, I didn't sleep a wink for 30 days. Sitting dope sick in a small cell, I'd think that 5 hours must have passed when it was only 10 minutes.

This was my new life. Puking. Freezing. Burning up. Shitting myself. Starting all over again. My roommate slept away most of the day, and I was left with myself. I had no books, paper, or pens. Since I'd started using as a kid, I'd never been alone. Now I was physically alone. Worse, I felt emotionally and spiritually alone, stuck with my own wretched thoughts. The only thing that broke through the prison of my own head was the piercing screams from other prisoners erupting day and night out of nowhere.

The highlight of my stay happened about every 10 days, when they would take me to another cell—one with a filthy, revolting shower. The only thing in my power I could do to feel alive was masturbate. So I did. It reminded me that I was still breathing.

Within a month, I started thinking and feeling for the first time in years without the cloud of alcohol or drugs polluting my judgment.

"I left Shannon and the kids without a dime."

Profound shame set in. I was a piece of shit. Just a few weeks before I'd begun my sentence, I'd cashed a check for $20,000. I'd planned to leave Shannon $15,000 to cover her bills. But I did what addicts do: I spent it all on drugs. I didn't leave her a freaking cent.

Years before, I'd reach for a drug or drink when I felt shame. Now I had nothing to comfort myself with except bitter tears. I'd spent so much time thinking about ME! ME! ME! that I'd had no thought for the people I'd hurt for years. In this cell, I had no space for emotions other than profound grief and regret.

We'd built our house in Oswego in 2002 while the economy boomed. In 2005, I took out a $100,000 equity loan on the house. I spent it all on drugs. By 2008, the market collapsed, and I quit paying on the house. It wasn't that I didn't have the money. I made plenty of money; I just didn't care about the banks. We sat in that house for four years without paying a penny. Now Shannon and the kids were in a house owned by the banks, and they were alone with no money.

Nick's words forced tears to flow down my cheeks: "Well, Dad, you're a *successful drug addict.*"

I was not a success. I was a liar. I was an addict. I was a fraud. I was a shitty father and husband. And I had no one to blame but myself, no one to curse except myself.

To add to my growing guilt, my wife and kids loved me beyond the moon. How could I look my kids in the eyes and say goodbye when their *hero* was going to prison? I'd abandoned them with nothing to keep them going. Why? Because I was a self-centered bastard and a drug addict. It was all about me. It had always been all about me.

As I lay there, something spiritual started to flutter in me for the first time. Some small spark ignited my dying pulse and replaced it with a slow, steady heartbeat. In this place of darkness, a shell without windows, a glimmer of light pierced the void.

I asked the void, "How can I get out of this dark place? How can I change my life? How the hell can I better myself so I'm never here again?" I had nothing to lose. Words from the past came back to me, and I finally understood that I'd just come to believe that a Power greater than myself could restore me to sanity.

I prayed awkwardly, like a construction worker trying ballet for the first time. Slipping out of my bunk to my knees, I prayed like I'd never prayed before:

"God, Higher Power, or whatever You are, please take away my obsession and compulsion to use, and I swear I will turn my will and life over to you. And please let me get to Sheridan Correctional Center..."

As I closed my eyes that night, Maggie Baker's face popped into my head, the girl I dated briefly in college and hadn't thought about since my first time in treatment. *One thing's for sure*, I thought to myself, *Maggie Baker has never seen the inside of a prison.*

I couldn't figure out why I was thinking of her. Then it dawned on me. I wanted the relationship with God that she had. I craved that relationship for myself. For the first time that I could remember, I craved something more than I craved drugs. Something was stirring inside of me that I hadn't felt before.

The next day, I learned that I was going to Sheridan.

CHAPTER 17
HOPE IS THE THING WITH FEATHERS

"Hope is the thing with feathers That perches in the soul, And sings the tune without the words, And never stops at all..."—Emily Dickinson

My dope was gone, my dope sickness was gone, and my will was gone. But for the first time in a while, hope had replaced dope in my life.

At 3 a.m. on my day of transfer, they came for me. *What is it about prisons and 3 a.m.? Do they ever do anything during normal business hours?* Then I remembered that much of my life outside prison kept the same backwards schedule. When I partied, many nights just started to pick up at 3 a.m.

While waiting to be loaded on the bus for the prison transfer, they locked me in a bullpen with the loudest, most obnoxious person I'd ever met.

"On my momma, keep the 100. On my momma..." he kept chanting like a fool.

God, keep this guy away from me, I begged.

For hours that nut job and I sat in that holding cell together.

One by one, guards took us fully shackled in chains and loaded us on a dingy, old bus with heavily tinted windows. They bolted our chains to the floor, so we couldn't do anything crazy, like hurt anyone or escape. I could see out the windows a little. I flashed back to the movie *The Fugitive*. I was living a life of the movies, just not one I'd pick out of a stack of choices.

While I took in the brutal reality of my surroundings, who do you think got seated and shackled in the seat right next to me? Yeah, Loudmouth from the bullpen.

Okay, God. I can handle a bus ride with this nut. But please, don't let him get off at Sheridan.

The bus lurched forward. I remembered that scene from *The Fugitive* when the bus wrecked and then got hit by a train. If the bus rolled over, they'd find our charred carcasses hanging upside down. As we exited the prison and entered the freeway, I looked out the window at the other cars: people headed off to work, kids going to school, and a few likely up to shenanigans. I thought about Shannon and my kids. It would take me two hours to get to Sheridan. *What were they doing now? What would they be doing when I got to Sheridan?*

I tried to tune out the yammering guy shackled next to me. Meanwhile people were striking up conversation.

"I got a five piece," one said.

"I got a year," another responded.

"Ya'll pussies," another boasted. "I got a 12 piece"

They went on and on like this was no big deal, just a way of life. And for many of these guys, it was a way of life. I knew I didn't look like I belonged there. I wasn't built like any of them. The heroin had reduced me to a bag of bones covered in grey, loose-fitting skin. Anyone glancing at my face would immediately know that I didn't look like this was just another day.

There was another guy behind me who didn't look like he fit in, either. He was sitting alone, and he was double shackled. "How much time you get, whitey?" one of the other guys asked him.

He turned, stared his questioner in the face, and said calmly, "*Forty* to life." The bus got silent for the first time, and all I heard was the whirring of tires going down the Illinois toll-way—the same toll-way taking women to deliver babies and men to job interviews.

"What 'd you do?" someone asked. It didn't matter who said it; we were all thinking it.

"I caught my girlfriend cheating on me. I cut off her head... and her boyfriend's head. Then I mailed them to her mom." He looked around at the others. A lot of eyes got very wide instantly. *Damn*, a voice said from behind him. *Damn, whitey.*

Loudmouth rocked back and forth while saying, "On my momma, keep the 100. On my momma..."

What the hell am I doing here? I thought.

I closed my eyes tightly and told myself that I could either let this experience kill me—or change me...for the better. It was change or die time for me.

I saw the prison outline against the blue sky from far away, as the bus lumbered through the gates. The bus would be stopping at a few prisons; Sheridan was the first stop.

They unlocked Loudmouth from the irons on the floor. At first I thought they were unlocking him so they could let me off. No such luck. They took Loudmouth off first, and then they came back for me.

God answers prayers, but not exactly in the way we expect.

With the dope out of my system and the worse of the dope sickness behind me, I remember almost everything from that first day. And that's unfortunate, because what I saw was painfully boring, depressing, and scary all at the same time.

We'd been on the bus for more than two hours. And then we waited. All the other guys seemed to know what was going on. I kept trying to peek outside without seeming like a rookie. We sat at the gate another 20 minutes, while they thoroughly searched the outside of the bus for contraband.

From my window seat, I could see all these people walking around like ants, some in baby blue jumpsuits, and others in nice, dark blue prison shirts with matching pants. It's funny I call them nice shirts, because I sure as hell wouldn't be wearing one outside those gates.

I laughed a little inside. *You're heading into prison, Tim, not a fashion show. What you wear should be the last thing on your mind,"* I reminded myself.

After what felt like an eternity, they hauled us off the bus like lambs to the slaughter. I looked out on the horizon and saw green grass. *It's a nice day*, I thought, as I scanned the blue sky. The ironic thing is, even though I'd be stuck in a cell, somehow it *did* matter that it was nice outside.

Sheridan was about 20 minutes from Skydive Chicago, a place I'd spent a lot of time jumping out of airplanes. Addicts are adrenaline junkies. Jumping out of planes provides plenty of that, making me feel freer than life itself. But in Sheridan, that freedom, that real world, was completely out of reach—even if it was only miles away.

When you jump out of an airplane, you need a parachute to bring you safely back to earth. And today, I needed feathers— wings, really—to transport me to a better place.

I scanned 360 degrees, taking in my surroundings. It was a far cry from the Chicago streets or Crystal Lake or anything I knew. Trees peppered my view, in between a cluster of small buildings I couldn't quite make sense of yet. Beyond the small ones, I spotted a couple of big buildings.

Once inside the prison gates, they unshackled us and walked us inside. I immediately smelled food and remembered how hungry I was. I'd been up since 3 a.m. Judging by the sun, it was around 11 a.m. when we got to Sheridan. They didn't exactly have attendants on the bus handing out peanuts and soft drinks, so I couldn't wait to get some chow.

This is where I'm going to spend a long time, I thought to myself. And then I remembered that guy on the bus. For him, this would be his home for the rest of his life.

That thought humbled me.

They gave each of us a property box. I opened mine up, flashing back to Christmas. I wondered what my kids were doing at that moment, as their dad unwrapped this small box of toothpaste, soap, and a couple rolls of toilet paper.

Inside that box, it was like I'd found a few feathers. Maybe even the makings of a wing.

You got an out date, Tim. You got an out date. Keep your eyes on the out date, I reminded myself. And I started doing that from the start. Even through the hell of everything, I started to turn everything into a positive out of the gate.

Thank You, God, for the toilet paper, I prayed inside my head. *Thank You for some hope.*

"Deuce it up, march it up, shut up," someone in a uniform yelled, and I knew it was time to move. They walked us down a sidewalk into a building called C7 that used to be the segregation hall. It was old and dingy. But it was going to be my home for the first 30 days, so I'd need to find something to like about it.

Loudmouth was right behind me, as we marched to our new barracks. I decided to pray again.

God, thank You for getting me into Sheridan. I won't let You down. I asked for one more chance to live, and You gave it to me. Thank You. Now can I ask one more favor: whatever You do, do not put this goofy guy in a cell with me.

That's when I learned that God has a sense of humor. Sure as shit, Loudmouth became my cell mate.

I learned something else: God does, indeed, work in mysterious ways.

117

CHAPTER 18
SETTLING IN

Guards led us into a very, very small cell—around 6 by 9 feet—with old, grey paint peeling off the walls. Honestly, it was the size of a walk-in closet, and inside I saw a little green plastic chair, a sink, a toilet in the corner, and two bunks.

Once the guard slammed and locked the cell door behind us, Loudmouth spoke: "Well, we might as well introduce ourselves since we gonna be bunkmates. My name is Qualo. And speaking of bunks, I like the top."

I didn't know what to think about God not answering my prayer regarding cell mates, but I had to admit it was nice to be on the bottom bunk. Being 6'1" with a bad back, climbing onto that top bunk would have been hard.

Since we were stuck in cells together until our permanent assignments, I needed to figure out who Qualo was. He talked a mile a minute. Qualo was no dummie, and he was no pushover. He was a stone-cold gang member.

"Look here, homey," he said, lifting up the back of his shirt. Dark little puckered scars from bullet holes covered his back. Qualo told me he was in for a drug conspiracy charge. He'd been a gang chief for 25 years. He was ruthless. I won't talk about the things he'd done, but he'd had 10 bids in prison for more than 25 years.

I grew thankful that God gave me what I needed and not what I asked for. Within 20 minutes, I knew I liked this guy. I really liked him. There was something about him that wasn't so different from me.

We shared so much so quickly after meeting that I forgot how hungry I was, until they opened our cell door and took us to the chow hall for lunch. A smell of heaven on earth filled my nostrils.

As we got nearer, my heart started pounding: *hamburgers.* I could eat the whole damned cow, I was so hungry.

Turns out they were soy burgers. But it didn't matter, because that was probably the best meal they served the whole time I was there. It just happened to be "hamburger" day. *Well, this ain't too bad,* I thought. *Thank You, again, God.* I needed hope. Those patties of pretend meat gave me another little dose of encouragement.

"Hey man, you gonna eat your fries?" a big guy asked the redheaded kid next to him. Next thing I know, people wanted me to trade food. Right out of the gate, I was oddly comforted by feeling that I was part of a system. I had street smarts, so I could present myself.

"Sure," I said, swapping for whatever the other guy wanted. I knew that if I were going to survive intact, I'd need friends on the inside.

As I chowed down, I eyeballed the guys near me. Some sat in groups, acting like they owned the place—and they probably did. Other guys shook like scared rabbits. One guy with tattoos down his arm sat staring at his food while bawling his eyes out as reality set in. His arms were tougher than his will, apparently. Prison isn't for a faint heart, that's for sure. I still didn't know what the hell would happen to me in that place, but I knew I'd do everything to survive.

After chow, we were herded to our cells again. I watched Qualo climb onto his bunk. His body was built like a shit brick house. Old power coaxial piping led to our dim lighting. After a short rest, that guy did 100 pull-ups on that pipe. He knew his way around a prison cell. I leaned back on the green chair, looking out the small window at the blue sky and sunshine, and thought, *how the hell did I get in here?*

But I got an out date, I reminded myself.

It turned out that Qualo would do around 500 pull-ups every day. He was always working out. I, on the other hand, weighed 158 pounds. I hadn't slept much for the whole month in Statesville. The drugs and fast lifestyle I'd lived for years had done a number on me, and I was skin and bones. When I was loaded, the man in the mirror looked to be in pretty good shape. In the dim light of prison though, I saw clearly that I'd become a walking skeleton.

That night, we were let into the day room for three hours. As I walked in, I absorbed my surroundings: a couple steel tables, a bench against the wall, a few chairs, and a TV. It wasn't much, but that room felt like a vacation. Hell, we'd do anything to get out of our cells.

That night, guys were sitting and playing cards and dominoes in the day room. Qualo's face lit up as he entered the room. Being a gang member, he knew a bunch of people. The rest of us non-gang members didn't feel very tough. It's hard to feel slick when you're dressed in a baby blue "Smurf" jumpsuit. It turned out that those "nice" dark blue uniforms had to be earned. These Smurf suit announced "fresh meat" to the entire prison.

When we came back to the cell that night, Qualo fidgeted like he had ants in his pants. "Man, check me out!" He took off his jumpsuit, and he had 20 ramen noodles, 10 envelopes, a handful of pens, and paper.

"What are you doing?" My eyes widened as I witnessed a display of what he materialized—in prison, of all places. He laid it out like we were in a convenience store.

"Bitch, I'm plugged!" he laughed, shaking a little. "I'm hooked up, bro'! I'm a gang chief, 'member? My people take *care* of me!" He placed special emphasis on the word *care*.

I thought of my grandma, Floey, and her cinnamon swirls. Those ramen noodles looked as good as a cinnamon swirl to me right now.

"And as my cellie, I'm taking care of you, too! Half is yours; half is mine." He sorted out the supplies, and I just watched. Two men from two totally different walks of life were bonded by the confines of a cell. Since he was affiliated, his people took care of him, and he broke bread with me.

This ain't gonna be too bad, I thought, for the first time in a while. Qualo knew how to make noodles on the heater without utensils. The guy was ingenious. That night, we shared chili ramen noodles and talked until 3 a.m.

When we finally stopped, I couldn't sleep. I flip-flopped around my bed like a dying fish, as the images of the day played through my mind. In the dark of the night, with no one's voice to break up the loneliness and desolation, all I could pray was: *God, help me learn what I need to learn here. And then, please, get me the hell out of here.*

CHAPTER 19

A BIG PERK IN A SMALL CELL

After about a week, I got a pin number for the phone. I waited in line for what seemed like hours, so I could call my wife and hear her sweet voice. Finally it was my turn, and even the sound of the phone ringing lifted my spirits.

"So I've landed, Shannon. I'm in some sort of holding area until they figure out what building to put me in. It's pretty bad, but I'm surviving." I waited for her to respond and cheer me up, but she said nothing. "Anyway, do you think you can put some money on my books? As it stands now, I have to beg or borrow to get anything."

There was a longer pause. "Tim, I don't have any money. So obviously I've got nothing to put on your books."

With no drugs in my system to numb me or make me feel like a rock star, I felt a fresh rush of shame. How dare I ask her for money when I'd left her with no money and all the bills?

But even as much as I'd wronged Shannon and let her down, she always found a way to help me, even when there was no way. This time, flat broke, she still managed to come up with $50.

After a little more time had passed, I called my mom. When I asked her for help, she paused. "Tim, you did this to yourself." I waited, sensing her wrestling with herself. "...You're my son...I'll give you $50 a month."

The prison commissary sold noodles, chips, honey buns, beef jerky, and other loot—and many prisoners spent the maximum there: $200 a week. A bag of tuna cost $2.99. My money wouldn't get me very far, but I was beyond grateful to have a full supply of ramen noodles. I never thought a stupid ramen noodle could lift my spirits, but that thing would fill my belly. I even gave some food to Qualo until he could get some money. I rarely visited that chow hall, because the food was crap. If I did go, it was just to move my legs.

My buddy, Aaron, became one of my heroes. He put 100 bucks on my books. I could buy a fan, some sweatpants, normal underwear—the simple things we take for granted. Money is the closest thing to freedom in prison, because it can buy things that remind you of the outside. Those comfort items remind you of better times—times when you felt alive.

Eventually, I chatted with prisoners in cells next to me. About two weeks in, I still couldn't fully accept where I was, but I had the routine down. Then I had another God moment. An older Puerto Rican gentleman transferred into C7. I walked up to him. "Man, I know you."

He looked at me, deadpan. "I don't know you from Abe, whitey."

"No, I never forget a face. I can't pinpoint it, but I know you."

"I've been down in Shawnee 12 years. You don't know me." Shawnee is a medium security prison about a six-hour drive south of Chicago.

I walked away, and about 10 minutes later, it hit me. I returned and said, "I know you. Cook County Jail, 2002—you used to run the deck. You're the guy who went outside the fence and brought in the drugs every day."

Finally, a smile creased across his face. "You're the white guy who borrowed my hand cream, and then we did a hit of X together. Yeah, I remember you." That was my inaugural trip to Cook County Jail for my second driving on revoked while struggling with heroin. I had used his skin lotion for my dry hands. This guy was sentenced on an attempted murder charge and in Cook County Jail for almost two years. He got 15 years total. He moved to Shawnee for 12 years, and with two years left on his sentence, transferred to Sheridan.

God was talking to me: *Tim, the first time you were in jail, you saw this guy. He's been in prison the whole 12 years that you've been slipping further into addiction. This doesn't have to be you.* Images of my babies' faces scrolled through my mind like an old movie. *Even though I'd drifted in and out of consciousness, at least I'd seen them grow. I'd earned money and walked as a free man.* Looking at the walls that enclosed me, it felt surreal that this man had been inside for so long. My gratitude muscle started to bulge; *it could be a lot worse for me.*

The next day, I walked to a school building. They checked to be sure we could spell right, draw with a crayon, and all that jazz. As I walked out of the room, I went up to the correction officer's desk. When he looked up, I said, "Hey, Mattress, how you doing?"

"My name is Officer Nickels. Go stand in the corner." I knew I'd done something wrong as I headed for the corner.

Five minutes later, Officer Nickels said in a hushed tone, "Hey Tim, jump out of any planes lately?" His nickname was Mattress. We sky dived together a number of years back. "Whatever you do, don't tell anyone in here you know me, because they'll kick you out. It's a security risk." My guardian angels were popping out of the peeling paint. Mattress stayed for another six months before retiring to work out of his house in another business. I almost wonder if he retired so I wouldn't get kicked out. Either way, awe hit me. *I know someone here.* He trusted me enough to talk like I was a human being and not just a prisoner. The edge of my loneliness dulled a bit into comfort. God had a hand on me, and He was showing Himself in unbelievable ways.

By this time, I'd stopped flirting with recovery. We were married. I leaned on my recovery as if it were the only thing keeping me safe, sane, and alive. And in a very real way, it was.

I went to group three hours a day, where they had three or four counselors. I was assigned to a lady named Miss Alayna. I learned to tell if counselor(s) were in recovery, or if they'd just studied it. I could tell Miss Alayna was in recovery herself.

"Where are you from in Naperville? Did you ever go to the West Suburban Fellowship Club?" she asked me one day. "Yeah, sure. Why?" I asked.

"Do you know Wallace A.? Or Lyle C.?"

It turned out we knew 40 of the same people. "I got sober there," she told me. By putting her in my life, God gave me a link to the outside world of recovery.

Later, she'd tell me, "I'm having dinner with Tom, and he said to say 'hi.'" That was another God moment for sure, that He put her in my life. My world was behind that fence. Miss Alayna reminded me that I mattered to life on the outside—that something positive could happen *after I got out*.

She also listened to my story. Finally, she challenged me: "I'll tell you what's wrong with you."

I leaned in expecting her to empathize with me or let me off the hook in some way, so when her words registered in my ears, I sat shocked a bit. But I needed to hear it, because I was at Sheridan to learn how to live free from addiction.

"You blame God for all your problems," she said, looking me up and down. "You're not surrendering to God. You're not living God's will." She paused, looking down at the floor before saying these words: "You know, Tim—Step 11—you really need to work on that."

Through the many years when I sat through meetings partially listening, I knew Step 11 by heart: *sought through prayer and meditation to improve our conscious contact with God as we understood Him, praying only for knowledge of His will for us and the power to carry that out.*

I can't say I understood what it meant to consciously contact God. Hell, I'd been driving my own life into the ground, and it sure didn't seem like God had been my constant wingman. But this lady seemed to know something, and I hungered for change. I started plugging in and participating by digging deeper.

I'd sit in small groups for those three hours a day, five days a week. Right away, I thought, *I can sit here like a fly on the wall, or I can plug in.* I found out in about two weeks that 90 percent of the 23 people in the group were really good people. It didn't matter what gang they were in; they just came from bad circumstances. I learned from these people. Some got jealous of someone, and there were a couple fights, but whatever. It was a game to some of them. Whatever you wanted to get out of it, you just stayed in your lane and did your own thing.

In the drug treatment program, certain protocol existed. We had to learn songs: the "Brother-Brother" song and "We're Here Because There Is No Refuge."

> *Until we confront ourselves in the eyes and hearts of others we are running. Until we share our secrets with them, we have no refuge from them. We can know neither ourselves nor anyone else. We will be alone. Where else but in our common ground can we find such a mirror? Here we can at last appear clearly to ourselves, not as the giant of our dreams, nor the dwarf of our fears, but as a person, part of a whole, with a share in its purpose. In this ground; we can each take root and grow, not alone anymore as in death, but fully alive in the midst of the world.*
> (Adapted from Richard Beauvais, "Pledge," written in 1965, while he was a resident in the original Daytop Therapeutic Community)

As I sang, I started to internalize something I hadn't really acknowledged before: *real hope.* My thinking shifted—from expecting something from the world to realizing I could walk with God, and He would stay by my side. I'd been calling hope any positive turn of event when, in reality, hope was always with me, because God was always with me.

And God needed to be with me. In order to get out of the ridiculous Smurf suits we wore as prison uniforms, I had to learn every word of those songs. With my learning disabilities, it took me more than a month. I could memorize five words a day. Sheridan housed about 1,700 people in their drug treatment program, and of those, I'd say about 200 to 300 were serious about recovery. When I finally got up and recited those words, those who were plugged into recovery clapped and clapped. Then a CO yelled, "Go get your blues, Ryan. You earned them!"

I was getting hope—one feather at a time. I transferred to the orientation hall. One huge building housed A hall, B hall, C hall, and D hall. All of A hall, which had 100 cells on the bottom and 100 up top, was the orientation hall. All I could think was: *I don't want to spend my time in a big ass building like this. I hope I can get transferred into the other cells in the little buildings.* With fewer people, the smaller units would have fewer fights.

I got placed in orientation, and Qualo ended up across the hall from me. A nice 23 year-old kid, Juan, was there. He called me Mr. Wrinkles, because of the way the sun had baked my face over the years. Talk about bad circumstances, Juan had worked at a factory making $16 an hour. He smoked weed. He'd never been in trouble in his life. He smoked a joint with his friend before work. His friend said, "Hey, pull in, I want to get an ice cream," before going into the shop. Minutes later, his "friend" ran out of the store with a drawn gun. He'd robbed the ice cream store, and a cop just happened to pull up behind. Juan got a seven-year prison sentence for armed robbery. Juan was good people.

I literally couldn't go anywhere. So I shut down many expectations and stopped being miserable about what I didn't have. I didn't expect phone calls with my family. I expected no mail. I expected no visits.

Instead, I relied on God to feed me during those dark hours. I looked for reasons to feel gratitude. If a letter came, it was an unexpected blessing. If I got that visit every two weeks, it was a gracious gift. If I called home and spoke to my family, it was a bounty. That's how I did my time, and that's how I started to transform my drive to use into a passion to live.

One gracious gift came when my former colleague visited me in prison. Prior to my incarceration, this friend had started a bad divorce. And now, as my friend sat across from me, he didn't even try to lift my spirits. Instead, he cried like a little baby: "Oh Tim, my wife left me. How could she do this?"

"Dude, it'll be good." I tried to reassure him.

Finally, he opened his eyes and looked up at me from his tears. "Hold on...God, I feel like an ass! You're the one in prison. Here you are helping me, and I'm the one crying!"

My motivation for reassuring him had changed: I didn't tell him that everything would be okay just to try to get him to shut up. No, I truly knew that things would be okay. Recovery had begun to take hold in me like a bursting seed. I started seeing the world differently. No one in the world owed me a thing; instead, I owed God everything. How could I complain when I had life, sobriety, a warm place to sleep, and food in my belly?

Mom and Dad came to visit me once. My people-pleasing nature kicked in. "I'm really embarrassed...I'm sorry you guys had to come see me here."

My dad looked up suddenly at me. "Embarrassed? You see that door over there? I walk out of there in two hours. You're here for the next year or two. Tim, you did this to yourself, and you're doing your own time—not mine." Embarrassment seemed too mild a word to describe his emotions.

When my time in orientation hall was over, I transferred to C21. God answered another prayer: I got assigned to a little building.

"Hey man, what's up?" I figured I'd try getting off on the right foot with my new cell mate. When he turned to look at me and stood up, I saw that this guy was the size of a small ship.

Looking down at me, the hulking figure asked me, "Hey, whitey—you into recovery?"

"Yeah, why?"

"If not, you ain't coming into this cell, brother, because that's all we do in here."

God had answered more prayers than the ones I'd uttered consciously. "Yeah, brother, I'm into recovery. Believe it or not, you, my man, are an answer to prayer."

"Well, good," he said, finally relaxing. "I'm Big Perk. Nice to meet you."

"I'm Tim." I shook his enormous hand.

"I think I'll call you Powder."

"You can call me whatever you want." Big Perk could bench press 400 to 500 pounds. He was not a guy I'd want on my bad side. That man became my best friend for the rest of the time I was in prison.

"My boy—my own son—got shot and killed on the West Side of Chicago two months ago," Perk told me. "He wasn't even no gang member. He was breaking up a fight, and some gang members lit him up." There were a couple of guys beating up a girl in front of a beauty shop. Perk's son, Hansen, spun them off and was consoling the girl, and some gang members came out and thought he was beating her up, shot him seven times, and killed him.

Over the next month, we cried about that, and we prayed on it. Meanwhile, I thought of Nick in his own prison of addiction.

My water skiing skills came by watching others and investing hundreds of hours in honing my skills. If you want to be okay at something, dabble; if you want to master it, invest. In that small cell, Big Perk and I invested. We studied the Bible, recovery books, books about business, karmic healing, cosmic energy, spirituality, etc. I read hundreds of books—checking out as many books from the library as they'd allow every two weeks. I consciously avoided watching television, because I wasn't there to pass time; I was there to grow as a person and child of God. I devoured Napoleon Hill, Tony Robbins, and Norman Vincent Peale.

After studying all day, Big Perk and I would talk into the wee hours about what God was teaching us. "Powder, man, I tell you… God put me here. I'd been in prison for a year and a half, and out of the 50 who wanted to go, mine was the only ass that got put into Sheridan."

God had given me a gift—by bringing me to this prison and putting me in this cell with this individual. Of all the people who I could have shared that time with, Big Perk was the one I needed.

I think we needed each other. We used our time like soldiers in boot camp. We needed to learn everything we could while inside the "safety" of prison, because the real test in the battlefield began once we'd get back on the outside.

One night as Big Perk and I talked, God planted an idea in my heart to start a recovery foundation for people in addiction. Big Perk liked my new vision, and it got him excited, too. "Powder… we gotta do something for the kids in the inner city. The gangs, the guns, and the drugs—these kids have nowhere to go." We shared silence and tears for the next several minutes.

Suddenly, he popped out of the bunk and said: "I've got it: H.A.N.S.E.N.—Help A Negative Situation End Nonviolently."

I wrote down every idea that came along, and that little seed of a thought began to grow as the days turned to weeks, and the weeks turned to months.

CHAPTER 20
BROTHERS IN ARMS

Hope grew inside of me like grasses on an Illinois prairie. And nothing amplified my hope—or shame—like visits from my family.

Shannon tried to come every two weeks with Abby, and she usually brought one of the boys along, too. Abby was a 12-year-old who craved her daddy. She was the blossom of my eye, but by this time, I'd taken her to hell and back. I missed her seventh and eighth birthdays, because I was in prison. By this time, the cat was out of the bag on most of my lies—at least the ones I could remember.

Meanwhile, Nick dove deeper into addiction, and seeing his dad in prison didn't help. The others hovered in the middle, trying to be good kids for their mom.

Penetrating that waiting room, seeing Nick and Abby through the glass, I wanted to embrace them hard enough to take away every rotten thing I'd done. *If I could go back in time, I'd become like my dad—reliable, loving, without the shit drama.* But I couldn't. And recovery taught me that the harder I tried to change the past, the farther I'd get from a healthy future. My life would have to become a living amends, starting with my real presence during those family visits.

During visits, prisoners sat at a four-person, steel table. I could never leave that seat. If I moved, they'd send me back to my cell.

In that cold, metal chair, nothing existed except my family. I shut out all the other guys in matching suits. I shut out the guards. I shut out the noises of the vending machines and chatter of other families.

Shannon left often to buy snacks. I don't think she craved a KitKat bar or Doritos as much as she needed a break from my reality. Plus, with something in her hands, her focus could shift away from my weathered, shamed face.

When Shannon returned, she gave the kids change to get something out of the machine. I'm sure they needed the break from me, too. When Nick left for some chips, Shannon's look got serious. "Look at his eyes, Tim. He's high. Nick is high right now."

My heart dropped to my knees. But how could I be surprised, given that I'd just recently gotten dead serious about my own sobriety? Knowing that Nick was in the same hell I had just left behind terrified me. Helplessness knocked me back like a huge breaker wave. As an addict, I only saw my own problems. I never fully appreciated how my selfishness had cost everyone else. But now my eyes darted around to the pain I'd caused my family. I prayed in that moment that Nick would follow me in sobriety, just liked he'd followed me into heroin addiction.

Nick returned, shifting in the slick, metal chair. Gazing into his eyes, they might as well have been mine. As my adopted son, he was just like me in so many ways—funny, full of life, high energy, street smart...and an addict. "Buddy," I said awkwardly, when his mom took Abby to the bathroom. "I can't be at home right now."

Nick looked up at me between crunches and snickered. "Ya' think?"

I exhaled, trying to push the shame out from the base of my lungs. "You know, your mom really needs you to be the man of the house. Your sister and brothers need you. I'm counting on you to step up and take care of the family." He smacked on his chips. "*Don't do what I did, son.*" I paused again. "*You've got to stay clean, okay?*"

Nick stared at a fleck on my prison blues, before catching my eye again and smirking. "Yeah, whatever, Dad."

The two hours sped by, and my family exited those cold doors again. I'd wait two weeks for another chance to see them, and in between, I'd focus on becoming better—instead of bathing in my shame. But I'd dip my toes in that murky water many times.

I lived for those visits, but each one was bittersweet. Updates about how things were on the outside didn't always help my state.

While I was in prison, time ran out on the foreclosure. We lost our beautiful dream house. I displaced my wife and kids. Shannon was left packing up that home all by herself with the three boys.

"We're living in a townhouse, Tim," Shannon told me. I felt like a big pile of steaming shit.

Hope, I told myself. *I have to focus on the hope, or the shame will kill me.* I'd finally made it to Sheridan. I knew my run was over, which was a relief. *I had an out date. This is the time to change,* I reminded myself.

I couldn't do anything about the outside world. But that doesn't mean the outside world was done doing things to me. "I don't know if I can do this anymore, Tim," Shannon said. I knew what she meant. What could I say? Nothing, really.

I got a book from the library on divorce. I knew one thing: I didn't want Shannon to divorce me. But recovery showed me that this decision wasn't in my hands. I wrote Shannon a letter to try to talk things through. She was done talking.

On Father's Day 2013, early in the morning, I called home from the dayroom. "Hey, Shan, you coming to see me today?" I missed my kids.

"Yeah, yeah, we'll be there," she said. She didn't sound thrilled. "I've got to tell you, Tim. I sent you a package."

Second best to having visitors was getting a package from the outside. My heart raced a bit. "Ooh, what did you send me? Some magazines? Some books?!"

"No, Tim," I heard her breath heavy against the receiver as she tinkered with something—undoubtedly breakfast dishes for the kids. I knew something was wrong. "I sent you divorce papers, Tim. I can't do this anymore."

Had Big Perk punched me in the gut, the air couldn't have left my lungs any more quickly. "I'm sorry," was all I could say. I couldn't argue.

Five hours later when she visited, I sat with her and Max and Abby, thinking about where it had all begun and where we were today. All I could think was: *I can't blame the lady.*

And I didn't blame her.

I had plenty of time in prison to process our divorce. I had two choices: I could let circumstances and my emotions take me out with the tide. Or I could keep my eyes to a point on the shore— and start swimming to it.

I would not wish prison on my worst enemy. At the same time, I needed prison to sober me up and give me a fresh perspective. Once I stopped my self-induced madness, I had time and a heart to pray, to ask God to reveal His will to me, to deepen my recovery. Today, when I'm working with a family of an addict and the addict is facing jail time, I remember my own experience: *you can use this experience to make you bitter or make you better.*

God continued to open doors for me and give me opportunities to deepen my desire to know Him and follow His will. This Cuban guy named Manny Mills, who had been in prison 28 years prior, ran ministries called Radical Time Out and Freedom God's Way. When you are in prison, you sign up for anything to get out of your cell. *Church retreat? I'm going. Ministry weekend? I'm going.*

I went to Manny's Freedom God's Way weekend. I felt like Manny was talking to me the whole time. At the end of the event, he stopped and said, "What is your name, and why are you here, my brother?"

"My name's Tim Ryan. I'm a drug addict and alcoholic. I got my third DUI..."

Manny interrupted me. "Tim, this is God's timeout for you. God sat you down here to reflect on your life. You can change, or you can go right back to the same life and be right back here."

Man, he was right on point. For how many years did I lie to myself and others, saying that I was *done using drugs* or *done drinking*? When times were hard, I reached for some form of self-medication; when times were good, I reached for the same self-medication. God had me where He needed me to be: in timeout. This is where I could get clean and sober, and this is where I could get honest with myself for the first time. I don't think that would have happened unless God put me in this timeout.

"My brother, Tim, would you like a book?" He handed me a paperback with *Radical Timeout* blazed on the cover.

Glad for any guidance, I met his hand and grabbed the book. Opening the cover, the first thing I saw inside was, "Crystal Lake, Illinois."

"Manny, what's this?" My weathered hand pointed to the words.

"Do you know the town?"

"Do I know the town? I grew up there! My grandfather built the first houses on the lake."

"That's where I was paroled to 28 years ago!" Instantly bonded, Manny asked, "Hey, when do you get out?"

"I don't know—nine months?"

"Well, we'll pick you up at the gate. I also do that."

"Thanks, man, but my ex-wife is coming to get me. I have that covered." I thanked him again for the book and his encouragement. Then I hurried back to my cell to read. Five hours later, I finished it. I immediately wrote him a letter of thanks.

About four months later on mail call, a letter came. It said "Quantum Executive Search." *Man, I must be getting sued for a bogus deal I did,* I thought. *I can't outrun my past!* I ripped open the letter:

> *Hi Tim, my name is Charlie Davis. My dear friend, Manny Mills, shared your inspiring letter with me. I'm a brother in Christ, and I'm praying for you. I'm also in the same industry, and I know who you are. If there is anything I can do for you, let me know.*

Some guy named Manny who I met once had shared my letter with one of his friends. That friend, a guy I'd never met, was willing to be there for me. And even more powerful to me was that he was praying for me. Addicts are takers. This guy was no taker. He was offering up prayers on my behalf, something that I'd begun to crave more than ramen noodles.

You know the saying, "A watched pot never boils?" Time passes more slowly when you're waiting for something to happen. And even though I knew checking off days in a calendar wouldn't make my prison time go or feel faster, I kept close watch as the days ticked down.

I won't go into all of the weird math used in the Department of Corrections, but that seven year sentence of mine got broken down into three charges: three years for DUI, three years for driving while revoked, and one year for possession of drugs— because of the spoon and syringe they found in my car after the wreck. These sentences were served concurrently, which meant I'd do 50 percent of that time. Plus, I got time taken off my sentence for being in a drug treatment program.

Most of the guys in my program had tried to get into Sheridan just because they could get time off for drug treatment and "good time." Plus, it was easier to get visits from Chicago. Most weren't at Sheridan to recover; they were just biding their time before drifting out again to the lives they'd known. I knew one thing: *I couldn't end up back here, or I'd die. And I couldn't end up back out there without a real change either. I had to take it seriously.*

From the time I caught my case on December 16, 2010, to the time I walked out of prison on December 16, 2013, exactly three years had passed. And those three years felt like a lifetime.

CHAPTER 21

A NEW DIRECTION

Even given all of the ways that I had let Shannon down, she met me at the prison gates on my release date.

I was supposed to be on parole for two years, but I was off in less than one because I was doing everything "right" and living a life of recovery. I also had to do TASC (Treatment for a Safer Community) probation and 25 hours of outpatient drug treatment. I blew that out in the first 45 days.

A month before I got out, Shannon had told me, "Your mom is willing to help get you a place. We have a couple of options." I could tell that one or two of them wouldn't work for her, but I was ready to listen. "She asked if we would all live together. She'll rent us a house in Oswego to get us all back together." Shannon waited before adding, "Tim, to be honest, I don't think I can do that."

Once again, I couldn't argue.

"Or your mom will rent a house for you and the kids, if that's what you want."

"Thanks, but I'm not ready to do that. As much as I love and miss them, I need some time on the outside alone to get my feet under me."

Shannon found a little townhouse in downtown Naperville. She chose it for three reasons: I could walk to recovery meetings, it was close to the train for work, and I could walk to downtown Naperville to shop.

Right out of prison, she took me to see my new place. She'd taken the time to set me up with some of the furniture from our home in Oswego. Gratitude hit me like a wave of euphoria. *I didn't walk out of prison to a halfway house. I walked into a beautiful townhouse in downtown Naperville with a chance to start over.* God was most definitely taking the reins in my life. I couldn't drive, I couldn't do much without a parole officer checking on me, but God held me close.

Shannon brought our kids over that night, and we ate Portillo's Italian beef sandwiches with cheese fries. That was the best meal I'd eaten in my life. I thought that Portillo's Italian beef and cheese fries must be a part of every meal in heaven. I recalled "hamburger day" in prison. Then I flashed back to hovering around the heater to chow down on Qualo's ramen noodle loot. *Boy, am I lucky,* I thought, looking at my kids, and thinking about Qualo, still in the joint. I felt oddly normal and good.

Besides eating the best meal I'd had in my life, I'd have no idea why that dinner was so significant until later. God was taking the reins in my life, but the battle horses still swarmed.

Four days later, Ramsey, my parole agent, took me to the 5 p.m. recovery meeting. A lovely, blonde lady sat right next to me. Her smile warmed my cold bones. "I'm Kirsten," she said, drawing me in.

Later that night, a friend took me to Manny's Radical Timeout group. "Tim, brother!" Manny's friendly voice boomed as he reached out his arms to embrace me. *My life was good.* I couldn't remember the last time I'd thought that.

I wasn't out of prison two days when I got a phone call from one of the recruiters I'd worked with who'd fired me. "Tim, I heard you're out of prison. What's your address?" I gave it to him and asked why. "Because I've been holding a check for you for $4,000 commission that I still owe you." He sent the check by FedEx.

If I hadn't put my feet in recovery, that check would have sent me to the West Side. But this time, I needed to do something with that money that wasn't all about me.

Christmas approached. I called Shannon. "I have something for you...It's a check for $4,000, and I need to give you half of it." I owed some of it for child support, and I wanted to make sure the kids could have a good Christmas that year.

Within three weeks, another consulting buddy of mine called. "Tim, I'm going to give you a shot. I want you to come work for me. We'll start a recruiting company through my consulting firm."

I walked to the 6 a.m. express train that took me from Naperville to Chicago, walked over to Ogilvie Train Station, took the 7:15 to Palatine, got in at 8:15, and hopped a cab or bus to the office. I worked my eight hours, then did that whole route back. It was a four-and-a-half hour commute each day. I made sure that I was back in time every night for the 8 p.m. 12-step meeting. Keeping a strict schedule every day helped my recovery.

As I slipped into a groove after prison, Nick slipped further off the tracks into addiction. One side of me longed to be back with Shannon, like maybe that could fix things that weren't working— but the other side knew I'd never been in a healthy relationship in my life. I didn't know how to do it, because I'd never been clean and sober. So the time alone was good—but hard.

My son, Tanner, wanted to be in Naperville, so he moved in with me. His presence brought me joy.

I didn't have much of a long-term goal, but I knew one thing: I wanted to stay sober. So I got a buddy, John, to be my sponsor— who was 21 years sober. He walked me through the steps again. Big Perk and I had done all that in prison, but I learned there was no limit to how many times I could do the steps and deepen my recovery.

A friend asked me to start a heroin anonymous meeting at his church, which I did. It quickly morphed into my first opiate recovery group—the first meeting in the area where families could come with the addicts. After all, addiction touches the whole village. Instead of working with the family one day and the addicts another, why not bring them together for a session and then separate them to do their own work?

I remember reading in Psalms, "Take delight in God, and he will give you your heart's desires." The more I sought to follow God's will and deepen my own recovery, the more my desires changed. And as I grew more invested in the recovery community, my passion for my day job vanished. Prison changed me. I worked as a recruiter for three months, and I hated it. I wanted nothing to do with that business anymore. God gave me a burning desire to help those trapped in addiction. I assessed all of the not-for-profits in the heroin space, hoping I could find a way to pay the bills while keeping my focus of helping others front and center.

I pulled out the notes I'd written in prison outlining the recovery foundation idea that God gave me. Pieces started to fall in place. Without even knowing it, God gave me more and more opportunities to begin converting those penciled-in notes into pen.

Meanwhile, when I was 19 months sober, Nick returned to drug treatment at Gateway. This was his fifth time in treatment. I had 25 hours of task probation to serve, something I did at Gateway. As I finished my rotation, I visited with Nick. I'd never felt more connected to my boy than during the hours we passed laughing and talking about some of the crazy things we'd done. We discussed recovery programs and ideas to make a difference in the opiate epidemic that was wrapping around our community.

"Dad, man, we could go tour the world!" Nick said with passion. "We've got a story like no other family. We'll go speak in high schools!"

As I left, I hugged him. Excitement flooded me walking out of that treatment center. Nothing felt better than imagining my son beside me in sobriety. Together, we could allow God to use our struggles for good.

Addicts are good runners, and sobriety sometimes chases an addict several steps behind until the addict falls flat and accepts no other way to live.

Nick got out, but 30 days later, he was in Cook County Jail. He and his girlfriend tried to sell bogus pills to buy heroin. Nick called me every day from jail, sometimes two to three times, and we talked like there was no time limit. I put money on his books. I knew how it was to be stuck with crappy jail food. I knew he needed some grub to feel human again.

It turns out, Nick traded all the food to get a prison tattoo on his arm: "YOLO—you only live once." That was Nick.

After 30 days in Cook County, Nick got transferred to Kane County for another case; he had OD'd and spit in an ambulance driver's face.

After he got released, Shannon sat him down over lunch. "We're done, Nick," she said. "You're not coming to my house, you're not coming to Dad's, and you're not going to Grandma's."

"Don't worry, Mom," he paused only for a second between French fries. "A buddy is picking me up. We got it all figured out!" It might seem odd to family members of addicts going through hell, but he did have a conscience. I truly don't think he wanted to worry us. And I know for sure that he didn't want to make us watch as he spun out of control.

By now, Kirsten and I had grown closer. She helped me set up my organization, A Man in Recovery Foundation. I'd researched other non-profits, and I felt that none of them focused enough on helping the addicts. That's all I wanted to do.

My mom loaned me $15,000 to live on and file a 501(c)(3). I surrounded myself with other business experts to help me in their areas of strength. In my mind, I'd get my foundation up, make a $40,000 a year salary, and save the world from heroin addiction.

I was naïve, to say the least. God held me close as I learned some of the hardest lessons of my life—including that sometimes the ones we love the most are the hardest ones to save.

CHAPTER 22
SAYING GOODBYE

Five days after Nick was out of jail, I called him. "Nick, come to my house and get Narcan. I'm a certified Narcan trainer."

Narcan is a drug that blocks the effects of opioids. It's also referred to as an overdose "reversal" drug, because if it's administered in time after an overdose, it can save a life.

"Dad, don't worry," he said. "I'm not on that bullshit anymore. I'm not doing heroin."

I believed him. In retrospect, I think I wanted to believe him, the same way a 10-year-old wants to believe in the Easter Bunny, the same way Shannon had wanted to believe me when I told her lie after lie.

Two days later, Shannon called me at 6:30 in the morning. I was in my townhouse sipping my coffee, contemplating how far I'd come.

"Nick overdosed again," she was breathing hard. "I'm coming to pick you up. He's at Hinsdale Hospital."

I threw on the closest clothes my arms could grab and waited outside my townhouse for her. At first, we went to the wrong hospital, Good Samaritan in Downers Grove. We couldn't think straight.

As we drove down the 88 expressway, Shannon's voice got shaky. "Tim, I know Nick has gotten out of a lot of jams, but this is different. I don't think this is good...I asked the nurses if they used Narcan. They said he was unresponsive." Shannon was a nurse, so she was no dummy when it came to the effects of heroin.

"It'll be okay," I told her. I wanted to believe my own words.

Nick told me that he wasn't stupid enough to use that shit anymore, but the last thing on my mind was any sort of judgment towards him. I just wanted to know that my little boy was okay.

To fill the silence, I plugged my iPhone into Shannon's car charger and looped it into her sound system.

The song "Courtesy Call" by Sixx:A.M came on my shuffle, a song about someone overdosing and dying. I yanked the phone plug out of the receiver. Shannon and I looked at each other, our faces white. We drove in silence.

All I could see was Nick's face. I started flipping through memories like they were a shuffling deck of cards. Nick was the happiest, most outgoing kid in the world. He was a younger version of me. And like me, he struggled with attention deficit disorder and was an insane thrill seeker.

Nick started skateboarding at 6 when I took him to RQ Boardshop in Naperville and bought him a brand new longboard. I taught him how to ride it outside our house on South Wright Street. Since we had no sidewalk, we rode in the street and dumped into the grass. We had two rules for him: wear a helmet and pads whenever on the board, and don't ride when I wasn't around. I was afraid for him, since he was only six years old and already fearless.

A week after I got him that board, Shannon and I went to Chicago to see the Titanic exhibit, leaving my mom to watch Max and Nick. Nick snuck that longboard out, and he bombed down the hill. A City of Naperville worker happened to be driving a city van up that hill while looking for a street address. He plugged Nick.

"Man, he went 15 feet in the air and landed on his head!" the driver told us later. If he hadn't worn a helmet, he would have died. Instead, he broke his femur in half and was scarred from head to toe.

When my mom called us to tell us about the accident, Shannon and I rushed straight to the hospital. Running inside, we found his room and burst through the door. "Dad, how ya doin'?" Nick asked, in his usual matter-of-fact way.

"Buddy, what the heck happened?" Relief filled me, even though he looked pretty smashed up.

"I snuck the longboard out." A look of both concern and awe crossed my face. *He was my boy.*

Nick started first grade in a wheelchair and learned to walk again. As soon as he was up on his feet, he asked, "Dad, where's my skateboard? I want to go out." Yeah, he was my boy. Since I couldn't keep him from adrenaline sports, I built a quarter-pipe in the back yard to encourage him to stay within sight.

Nick loved life and his family. The first time I took him water skiing at nine years old, I taught him to barefoot ski in no time. Nick was athletic, Mr. Outgoing, and a free-spirited kid.

He was also a friend to everyone. When we moved to Oswego, Nick started hanging out with this kid, Carlos. At 12 years old, he and Carlos delivered marijuana for Carlos' older brother, a Chicago gang member. They got arrested for spray painting some playground equipment and had to face charges. We came out of court and our attorney, Fred, looked at him. "Nick, you've got your first two felonies."

Nick shrugged. "Well, I did it." And it wasn't the last thing he'd do. Once caught up in the court system, Nick never got out. Shannon and I went to court with him nearly 100 times: underage drinking, possession of marijuana, getting kicked out of high school for drinking and smoking weed. He finally got a settlement from that car accident when he was a kid, so when he turned 18, he got more than $20,000. He burned through that in six months. And he got a DUI—under the influence of heroin.

Yeah, Nick was my boy.

As I sat in Shannon's car, racing towards our son, I thought about how I'd done nothing to support his recovery through most of his troubled teens. *How could I?* I'd been in worse shape than he was.

The hospital EMERGENCY sign shuddered me back to the present. Shannon and I parked and ran into the ER. I couldn't wait to get into his room and hear him say, "Dad, how ya doin'?" But my legs felt heavy running through those glass doors, like they were pulling me backwards.

"Tim and Shannon Ryan, here to see our son, Nick. He overdosed." The woman at the front desk punched some keys on her computer. About 30 seconds later, a female chaplain walked out of a room and stopped in front of us. Such a thing might seem innocent enough that a typical bystander wouldn't even notice it, like a leaf falling from a tree overhead. But to me, this felt like an omen. *Let me talk to a doctor, or anyone but a chaplain. A doctor can tell me what we need to do now that my son is okay; a chaplain can only try to hold me up when my world collapses.* My mind was screaming, but I couldn't speak.

In that moment, the hospital lights seemed to gray out overhead. The waiting room turned into a tunnel I couldn't escape. The people nearby looked mechanical. The chaplain led us into a back room. Shannon said nothing, but both of us thought the same thing: *when are we going to see our son?*

A doctor in a long, white coat entered the conference room where Shannon and I waited. Getting to the point, I asked, "So what's up?"

A well meaning voice full of compassion asked one of us, "Did you know your son struggled?"

I thought of my long battle with heroin addiction—my yo-yo ride, my crash, my ride to prison. I thought of lying in the bathtub, dope sick, and seeing Nick's face like the angel of life—or death, I couldn't tell which.

"Yeah, we knew he was a heroin addict," Shannon said without breath or eye contact. What else could we say?

I could tell by the doctor's hesitation that he had something else to say. The earth spun so slowly, I thought it would stop. And part of me wanted it to, so I could hold onto what I knew.

"I'm so sorry. Your son didn't make it." Shannon fell to the cold floor on her knees. A deep silence fell as she took a breath in, and the whole room froze. If the earth had stopped, Shannon's piercing scream set everything in motion again. Faceless people rushed in to console her, which was impossible.

"I'll be back," I said, squeezing her shoulder. I walked out into that hallway and entered the room where the chaplain had exited, two doors down. There was my beautiful son's lifeless body, ice cold, with a tube coming out of his mouth. The machines were off. There were no sounds of breath, no sounds of life.

A wave crushed me, but I was still standing. *What had I done? I set all this in motion. I helped kill my own son with my shitty example. I'd shown up too late.*

I don't know how long I sat with my son's cold body as tears fell down my face. Eventually, I returned to the room with Shannon. She looked up at me, a glimmer of hope in her eyes, praying that the doctors were wrong or that the hospital admissions had messed up and admitted the wrong kid. When she saw my face, that hope disappeared. I couldn't reassure her that it was okay. *No one could. It was not okay.*

"Yeah," I said. "It's him. He's gone." She fell into my arms and sobbed, moaning and screaming like a mother in labor. I stood her up, holding her by the shoulders, my arm squeezing her slightly. I turned and guided her into Nick's room. I watched as the mother of my children sat in a chair at the foot of our son's body and wept— for a life she couldn't touch. *It was over.* My battle with heroin ended in recovery; Nick's battle ended in death. *His addiction killed him.*

Years ago when I'd first gone out with Shannon, she'd scanned my face in a restaurant and asked me point-blank with a slightly insecure smile on her face, "Do you do drugs?" I lied to her as naturally as breathing. And now my oldest son was dead in front of me; Shannon vacillated between weeping quietly and wailing loudly, stopping only long enough to suck in more air.

What had I done to her? Grief and guilt pounded me like a rogue wave. Nick died on my 21-month sobriety date.

An instant, overwhelming urge hit me. For more than 30 years, I'd used drugs to deal with any emotion. This time, *I need to be at a meeting tonight*, automatically popped into my head. Since I'd started praying, God had been taking over my heart. He was slowly replacing my drive for a quick high with a *longing for recovery and redemption*.

But before I could attend a meeting, I had people to call. I needed to stay active. I needed to run around the reality of the situation for a while and face it more slowly. That's what shock is: it's a gift.

I called my pastor, Bob; Mom and Dad; and Shannon's family. I tried to get Max, Tanner, and Abby there to say goodbye to their brother, but like most kids their age, they were scattered all around with activities. Eventually I tracked them down, and they agreed to come.

My mom came with Tanner, and I escorted them into the room. *How do you walk your son into the room where his big brother lies dead?* His tears over his brother's body triggered more shame in me. Tanner didn't deserve to hurt like this. I wanted us all back together, eating another meal of Portillo's as a whole family. I wanted to talk to Nick one more time, to tell him that God was stronger than any drug. I wanted a do-over on the 30 years I spent chasing drugs. I wanted my family to be intact, my kids to be safe, and Nick to be alive.

The words of Richard Beauvais I learned in Sheridan came back to me in a flood: "We are here because there is no refuge, finally, from ourselves. Until we confront ourselves in the eyes and hearts of others, we are running."

I had no choice but to face every bit of my past as this moment threatened to rip my heart in two.

The three kids who drove Nick to the hospital waited outside the hospital. His girlfriend, Madeline—who I'd only seen a few times maybe—Andy, and another kid were there. Gentle sobs jolted from them. "He's dead," I told them. They didn't seem surprised.

Nick had been dead about four-and-a-half hours prior to my arrival at the hospital. He was starting to aspirate, and the coroner wanted to come get him. Max and Abby were all the way in Oswego, working their way to the hospital. I called them and canceled their trip, because I didn't want them to see Nick the way he was with lung fluids streaming out of his mouth.

Nick died on Friday, August 1. That following Thursday, I was supposed to help lead a big Narcan training event at Wheatland Salem Church. Denise Crosby from the *Chicago Sun-Times* planned a big article in the paper. She caught wind of Nick's death.

"Tim, I'm so sorry," the concerned voice on the other line said. "I'll pull the story."

"Absolutely not. If they'd had Narcan, Nick might still be with us. Go forward with it," I begged her.

"Do you mind if I talk about..." she paused slightly before continuing, "this?" I knew what she was asking. She wanted permission to go public with my story. She felt genuine concern for the kids caught in this epidemic.

Gratitude flooded me again. *This woman with a voice wanted to tell the truth about addiction. Maybe I couldn't help Nick, but that didn't mean his death couldn't help others.* "Denise, please tell the story. It needs to get out."

She published, "Anti-Heroin Crusader Loses Son to Overdose," on August 4, 2014, in *The Courier News*—the first of many articles that would involve me, my foundation, and the kids who were chasing or running from heroin.

I went to my recovery meeting the night Nick died. I had to. My buddy, Bobby, came with a bunch of people down from Crystal Lake. Bobby had also lost a son to addiction. That's where I needed to be, with my recovery family.

Two days later on a Sunday, I attended a speaker meeting. A woman named Tiffany spoke. I'd seen her before, but I couldn't remember where. "On Friday, I was two years sober, and it was the worst day of my life." Her voice cracked as she started. "I got into it with my boss, and I said, *F-it, I'm going to drink.* I left work and was driving down I-88 when I got a flat tire. I thought, *Unbelievable! I'm SO going to drink!*" She paused. "For some reason, I went to the 6 p.m. meeting before hitting the bar. I was the first one to talk, and I shared my story of how my day sucked so bad that I was going to drink. I sat down almost daring someone to challenge me. Then a man shared that his son had just died from a heroin overdose that morning. What he shared humbled me instantly. I thought my problems gave me an excuse to go drink, and here he'd just lost his son. That man checked me on my recovery right there and then. I never went to the bar."

God had not only kept me clean and sober that night by giving me a burning desire to attend a meeting, but he'd also used Nick's story to help another soul deepen her own recovery. God was good, even when everything seemed horrible.

A few days later, we held a celebration of life for Nick at church. Around 800 to 1,000 people showed up. About 400 were people Nick or I knew from treatment or recovery. I could feel the tension with Shannon's family; they all blamed me for Nick's death, and they told me as much. After the funeral, I asked Max, Tanner, Abby, and Shannon point blank: "Do you guys blame me for Nick?"

"Dad," Abby began. "If this had happened two years ago, yeah, Dad. But you're 21 months sober." I didn't deserve such forgiveness.

For how long had I considered myself unstoppable, invincible? Nick was my boy. He thought nothing could hurt him, too. But after snorting two bags of heroin and eating a bar of Xanax, he lost his battle. He never used a needle. Most people have this picture of a heroin addict as a troubled kid in a dark alley with a needle in his arm. But that's often not the case. Nick was anyone's kid—my kid—and he could have been yours.

Nick would give you the shirt off his back. He was the life of the party. Nobody disliked Nick. He was there for his friends, and unfortunately he followed some of them into death. And some of them would likewise follow Nick into death. Nick was the 16th person to die of a heroin overdose in DuPage County that year; he wouldn't be the last.

The best way to get through grief and guilt is on your knees. I prayed for strength to follow God's will, whatever that might be. God was forming a song in my heart. My compulsion with alcohol and drugs was no longer playing the leading role. My latest high no longer took center stage. I shifted my spotlight to hitting the streets. My new role was to deal hope and unlock the same shackles on other people's souls that had trapped me and snatched my son.

PHOTO ALBUM

*The following photos depict my
family and me doing normal things.*

*Besides putting pictures to the faces I'm
telling you about in this story, I hope you see
in them a bit of yourself or even your family.*

*I hope this helps illustrate that
addiction touches people of all types—even
those who have fun together, go on family
vacations, and do sports. We look like the
most typical family on earth, don't we?*

December 2, 1993 - August 1, 2014

A Celebration of the Life and the Life Eternal

Our beloved Nick's memorial photo, 2015

Nick doing what he does best at Oswego State Park

Nick all smiles at home in Naperville

Max's 5th birthday party with all his siblings

Cherished family vacation at Venture Out in Florida Keys

Max, Abby, Tanner, and me at home in Naperville

A MAN IN RECOVERY

Nick with our dog, Cabo

Nick and I charter fishing on Lake Michigan

Christmas at home with the kids and Cabo

Tanner, Max, and Nick on the quarter-pipe we built for Nick

Abby, Max, Nick and Tanner enjoying popsicles at Naperville house

Our family at a skydiving event, North Avenue Beach, Chicago

Nick learning to water ski like his pops at my parents' house, 2002

*Tanner, Max, and Nick playing with their
wheels in our Naperville driveway*

A MAN IN RECOVERY

Nick and I in cub scouts, 2001, Naperville

Hay ride at a pumpkin farm with all the kids and Shannon, 2002

*Nick wanted to go to work with me one day, so I
let him (complete with a jacket and tie)*

Nick, Max, and I lying on basement floor of our house

A MAN IN RECOVERY

Tanner at swim practice

Nick barefoot water skiing like a pro

Kids with mixed level of enjoyment over canoeing
on lake at Grandma and Grandpa's

Papa (my dad) taking them out on a sailboat in 2003

Millennium Park, Chicago

Kids playing "King of the Raft," 2002

My beautiful children enjoying the summer at my parents' house

Tanner, Abby, me, Max, and Kirsten in 2015

CHAPTER 23
SWEET AND SOUR

When I first went to treatment, my goal had been to learn to drink and use drugs like "normal people." It wasn't until I went to Sheridan that I admitted to myself that I had no normal in me. I could use, or I could die. Up until Sheridan, I held this thought in the back of my head, telling myself, *Oh, I'll get Shannon off my back or get this new job, then I can drink like a normal person.* But once I truly surrendered my heart to the disease—and to the best of my ability got humble and started living God's will instead of Tim's will—the desire to drink and use drugs lifted. And the doors to help others started opening.

About two weeks after Nick passed away, Shannon met me at Potbelly's in downtown Naperville. In between bites, she said, "Tim, for once in my life I am behind you 1,000 percent." That was a lot coming from her, given that she was a wise woman, and I was often in trouble.

"What do you mean?"

"I want you to move forward with your foundation and help people. I don't want any parent to go through what we've been through. Heroin took my beautiful house; it took you, my husband; and it took our firstborn child. I truly believe God put Nick and me in your life for a reason. You went through all your struggles, and so did Nick—to unfortunately set the stage for what you're going to do next. *Now keep doing it.*" Shannon knew my drive to deal hope to others in addiction. The years that my addiction destroyed would serve as my training ground.

Around that time, Nick's best friend, Abe, got out of treatment. He'd been living in a halfway house called the Normandy House in Des Plains. They let him attend Nick's funeral. Abe was like a big brother to my kids, because he was just the nicest kid, and he'd been around our family for years.

"I'm speaking next week at the Alano Club," I told Abe. "I'd love to have you there." Abe took the train out to hear me speak.

Afterwards, I said, "Tanner's living with me, let's go over and visit him." When Abe walked into my condo, Tanner immediately hugged him.

"Where are you living?" Tanner asked.

"I'm in a halfway house."

Tanner shook his head. "Forget that, move in with my dad and me." That day, we packed up all of his stuff, and Abe moved in. I didn't realize how much I needed him there. Abe was like a sober son to me, a second chance.

At the same time, things grew more serious between Kirsten and me. We were living together and expecting a baby.

I started going to recovery meetings with Abe, and he got this guy, Wes W., to be his sponsor. Wes W. was an old hardcore dope head and former felon who would make Abe meet him at the club every day at 6 a.m. Like clockwork, Abe dragged his butt out of bed.

I introduced Abe to this 19-year-old girl, Jessica, at the Starbucks coffee shop. Next thing, they fell in love. Not long after that, Jessica was living in my basement with Abe. Abe did odd jobs, worked at Portillo's, and then washed dishes. He rode a bike his mom had given him. He was in front of the house one day with his blue jeans, a white tee shirt, and a cigarette. I took a picture, "Tim, I'm James Dean!" Abe joked.

"James Dean drove a Porsche, Abe—not his mom's bike with a basket," I responded.

We all laughed like family, because Abe was like my son while also being my brother in recovery.

About six months later, we were at the club, and Wes W. said, "Okay, how about we meet tomorrow at noon?"

Abe said, "Hold on, we meet at 6 a.m. every day."

"Right. But from now on, we'll meet at noon."

"Why?"

"I just had you meet at 6 a.m., because I wanted to see if you were willing to go to any length to stay sober," Wes W. told him. "Only an idiot or a guy committed to recovery would get out of bed to meet at 6 a.m. each morning. So let's do noon from now on."

During this time, A Man in Recovery Foundation grew. I started assessing treatment centers and figuring how could I get people into treatment more quickly A lot of them were nervous of me, but then I started referring people.

I stumbled into a place called Banyan Treatment Center out of Pompano Beach, Florida. Taylor Glenn, the director of business development, was trying to meet with some interventionists in Illinois, and they kept saying, "You need to meet Tim Ryan. He's very plugged into the heroin addiction and treatment communities." I met with Taylor for an hour and a half at Starbucks.

They flew me to Florida a few days later to see the operation. I loved what I saw. Out of 250 employees, I'd say 210 were in recovery—a bunch of young people helping young people. It seemed to be a very well-oiled machine. I respected most of the treatment centers in the country. But Banyan would let me keep someone in treatment three to six months versus the three to four weeks that most places allowed. I believed in what they were doing and how they treated clients.

They offered me a job on the spot to serve as their Midwest outreach director. *Me*, I thought, *an ex-con, recovering alcoholic, and heroin addict? They want me to work with them?*

God is good.

At Banyan, I started to see success when someone would stay at our program for four months and move on. I didn't send everyone to Banyan though, because not everyone was a fit. I'd refer some to other centers throughout the country. My goal was to help anyone get sober in the best environment. Most places don't have staff who will place someone in another facility.

Besides my Banyan work, 90 percent of my team's work remained for A Man in Recovery Foundation—of which 100 percent of the proceeds went to help people get treatment.

When Abe was about 10 months sober, I sent him to Florida with Jessica to work for Banyan as *behavioral health techs*. Abe and Jessica drove kids to 12-step meetings, worked in housing, and learned the ropes to get experience, until they were ready to return to Naperville and help Banyan open an office there.

Five months later, Banyan opened their new facility in downtown Naperville, and Abe and Jessica returned to handle all of our admissions. It felt like home to have Abe back, plugged in, and working alongside of me.

The operation quadrupled in size within 16 months. Banyan planned to open a state-of-the-art detox. The blessings were pouring in for me. Recovery wasn't sucking.

A month later, on August 27, 2015, my baby girl, Mackenzie, was born, and wonder re-entered my world. This baby became the biggest spark of life to anyone she met.

God called Nick home, and nothing could replace him. But God blessed me with another beautiful child, and I gained the gift of being able to raise that child 100 percent clean and sober. Getting up and changing diapers and all the things a father is supposed to do that I'd pawned off on Shannon—*I would finally get to do*. I was blessed, because of this gift of sobriety.

Abe and Jessica moved across the street from our Banyan facility in Naperville. Their old Victorian house was in full view from any of the Banyan rooms. My cellmate, Big Perk, was out of prison by now, and he came out to serve as my nanny right after little Princess Mac arrived.

Would you let an alcoholic, drug addict, and felon watch your infant daughter? How about one who'd committed acts of violence? How about one who was the size of a ship? We tend to measure others by their biggest failures instead of the amount of grace they claim. Big Perk and I had been saved out of a life of abusing alcohol, drugs, and others. No criminal watched my dear, sweet daughter; a godly man committed to daily recovery did. Big Perk remained my brother in Christ and recovery. I trusted this man with my life and most precious loved ones.

The interesting thing about Big Perk is, he had five brothers and sisters. They were all college graduates, very successful. He's just the one who chose to get into the gang life, and that's all he knew. When he got out of prison the last time, Big Perk took a train from University Park to Chicago, from Chicago to Naperville, to go wash dishes for ten hours for nine bucks an hour—before taking it back again. He commuted about four hours a day. He was willing to work. Something he said at that time resonated with me, when I mentioned the trouble he went through for that job: "Tim, when I used to sell crack and stuff, we were making 100 grand a day. At 19, I owned a couple restaurants." He went on, "But the first time I appreciated money was in 2008, when I got out the eighth or ninth time. I got a job at the Chicago Transit Authority washing buses and trains at night." He paused, "I got my first paycheck for two weeks for $300," and he said that was the first time he had ever earned money. "So no, I don't consider it any trouble to earn my living. It's a blessing."

Recovery isn't a magic pill that fixes every broken thing. The Big Book tells us recovery can offer us a "daily reprieve," as long as we invest daily to spiritual growth.

On December 9, Abe asked, "Hey, do you mind if I borrow the truck? I can give it back tomorrow." It was the company vehicle, and I couldn't drive it anyway given all my offenses.

"Sure. Why?" I asked.

"I want to go to a 12-step meeting." I didn't think anything about it.

The next day, on December 10, Jessica and I bustled about the Banyan office. Abe stayed home sick, which was unusual for him. Around lunch time, Jessica crossed the street to check on Abe. Five minutes later, Taylor, one of our clinicians, ran in and said, "Get across the street with Narcan! Abe's overdosed!"

I hesitated. "That's not funny!" I told her.

"Tim, I'm fucking serious." My blood chilled. I grabbed the Narcan, ran across the street, and sprinted up the stairs. Jessica was wailing, and my second son was lying there dead with a needle still in his hand. We hit him with Narcan six to eight times and started performing CPR, but it was too late. Abe had been dead about two hours.

Abe, like so many recovering addicts, thought he could use one more time. Like many others, that *"just one more time"* killed him. A large number of those who die from an opiate overdose are coming out of treatment or jail—or they'd stopped using for a while. When they relapse, they go back to using like before they'd stopped. Their tolerance drops very, very quickly. My son, Nick, was locked up for 45 days, and when he got out, he went right back to snorting two bags of heroin mixed with Xanax. His body couldn't take it. It killed him. Likewise, Abe's body was no longer used to the drug, and even if it had been, it could have taken his life. *Heroin is never safe.*

Abe, the young man who helped check people into treatment, was carried out on a stretcher. Across the street at Banyan, those attending group therapy for their own drug addictions watched the entire scene unfold from the large windows. *How many of them would end up like Abe?* For some, it was a sobering scene, in the most literal sense.

I entered a state of shock and disbelief. Nick had never really grasped recovery. But Abe had. He was 17.5 months sober. I shattered like a fragile mirror tumbling down a staircase. Old wounds that had only started to scar over ripped open.

I learned later that Jessica had caught him huffing a month prior. "Why the hell didn't you tell me?" I asked.

"Abe didn't want to tell you, because you would have been disappointed. He didn't want to let you down." And I'm guessing he didn't want to lose his job, either.

In recovery, you are as sick as your secrets. Abe held onto that secret, and for whatever reason thought he could use heroin one more time. It killed him.

I couldn't help, because I didn't know. And even if I had known, Abe had to want recovery for himself more than I could have wanted it for him.

What Peter wrote in the New Testament about "the devil" could easily be changed to the word "addiction" and still speak complete truth: *"Your enemy [addiction] prowls around like a roaring lion looking for someone to devour"* (I Peter 5:8).

Lasting recovery is daily recovery. Addictions often play a waiting game with us, sitting back in the shadows and lulling us into a false sense of security, so they can pounce on us when we least expect it.

CHAPTER 24
THE MEANING OF FORGIVENESS

About two and a half months after Nick died, I was running one of my support groups on a Tuesday night at Wheatland Salem Church in Naperville. We'd come to the point in the meeting where we split up addicts and their family members into separate rooms. That night, I stayed with the addicts. After about 10 minutes, I stopped in my tracks and looked at this kid. "I never forget a face. Where do I know you from?"

"Um," the boy stammered. "I knew your son, Nick."

"Really? Did you party at our house or something?" I pushed him.

"Um, no," the boy shifted a little in his seat under my stare.

Then it hit me—the hospital, Nick's death, the kids that brought him in. My blood began to chill again. "My son died with you." Our eyes remained locked.

"Yeah, I met you at the hospital. My name is Andy. Your son died at my house."

I sat back in my chair and let out a long breath. I hadn't heard from Andy since Nick's funeral. Today, Andy was holding his breath, waiting for my reaction.

"It took a lot of stones to walk in here. You don't know me very well, and you don't know what I'm capable of doing." At that moment, I'm not sure that I knew what I would do.

"I know, but you're a good person, and I need your help." Andy kept eye contact.

"Before I consider helping you, I need the truth. What happened to my son?"

Even though I'd been trying to pour all my energy into helping others and putting the demons behind me, I needed to hear this. I needed to know what had happened. I needed some sort of closure. That's all I was thinking when I asked Andy to tell me the story. But remember, this was in the middle of a session full of other drug addicts. Even when I didn't know what I was doing, God had my back. These addicts were able to hear, see, and feel another side of the pain—that of *others*. I felt the effects while in the throes of my addictions, but it rarely occurred to me to think what I was doing to others. These addicts witnessed that night that they weren't just characters in a video game who could be reset back to life.

Andy inhaled deeply before starting the story of how Nick died. "Nick and Madeline came to my house. My parents were out of town. We were snorting heroin and drinking." He paused. "I gave your son a bar of Xanax." He paused again, looking at me for a reaction. I stayed stiff in my chair. "Nick ate it, and about a half hour later, Nick started overdosing."

"What did you do?" My question came out as a clipped, nervous statement, and I wasn't sure I wanted to hear the answer.

"Nothing…Well, we propped Nick on the sofa and went into the basement. We…we did more drugs. We came up like an hour later, and Nick was dead." His brutal honesty stunned me.

"You let my son die." It wasn't a question, but he answered it anyway.

"I let your son die."

"Why didn't you call 911?"

"Man, we panicked. We had a house full of drugs, and we didn't know what to do. We didn't know about Narcan." Andy searched my face for forgiveness before saying honestly, "I don't have an answer."

"Well, I saw you at Nick's funeral," I said, buying myself time to think about my response. "What have you been doing since then?"

"The day after Nick's funeral, I checked myself into treatment. I did a 30-day program. I'm now living in a sober home, but I'm not grasping this thing called recovery."

In Sheridan, after the drugs were completely out of my system, I spent hours at night grieving over all the people I'd hurt, disappointed, or let down. Of course I told my parents, Shannon, and my kids how sorry I was for being such a shit for so long. But saying, "I'm sorry," is not the same as making amends. Making amends means being willing to fix the damage. How could I fix the damage I'd caused my parents? Shannon? My kids? Nick? I couldn't. But I could make a living amends by living a different life.

I had a decision before me. I could throw this kid out on his ear, or I could pray and offer my hand to this enemy. "What can I do to help you?"

"Would you be my sponsor and take me through the 12 steps?" Andy asked.

The old Tim, Tim-the-addict, would have choked the shit out of this boy in front of me. That Tim no longer controlled me. Thank God l was a new Tim—one under His control.

"Of course," I told him immediately.

Andy and these other kids were destroying their own lives with their addictions, their friends' accumulating deaths, and the racking up of crimes in an endless spiral of despair. I didn't want to see another loss.

If you haven't been around heroin or those who use it, you might not have an accurate picture of the heroin addict. Most of today's heroin addicts are just like Nick, Abe, and Andy. They are in their young 20s—and many of them are female. They are middle class kids in good neighborhoods with good parents. They are the honor students, athletes, and girls next door—the last ones you'd suspect.

None of these kids say, "Hey, I think I want to try heroin," out of the blue. That would be stupid, and these aren't stupid kids. But many addicts have underlying mental health issues that go undiagnosed, whether it's ADD, dyslexia, depression, bipolar, or anxiety. They are running from some kind of pain, and they run to destructive drugs.

Some go to doctors and get a prescription to help them. Unfortunately, many doctors over-prescribe or mis-prescribe drugs. With opiates, doctors often prescribe pain medication for dental work, a broken bone, or other injury. When kids (or adults) start taking the medication, they feel relief—not just from their physical pain but also from their emotional and spiritual pain.

If you have a teenager, ask this question: "If you wanted Xanax or Oxycodone, would you know where to get some?" When I ask this in school assemblies, almost every hand goes up. Your kids know where to find drugs. They are everywhere.

Here's a story I've heard more times than I can count. A kid gets prescribed Xanax to help him cope. Or the kid hears about Xanax and buys some off a "friend." The medication helps the child feel less anxious. But what's the cost? Many times, the anxiety flips to the other extreme of recklessness. Now that kid's at a party smoking some weed and having a few drinks and feels bulletproof. Inhibitions drop away. Then someone offers, "I've got something for you to try that is going to rock your world," and pulls out a bag of heroin. Remember, this kid feels invincible. He tries it. He likes it. It's cheap, too. One pill of oxycodone on the street will cost $20, but a bag of heroin is just $5.

Not long after that, heroin becomes a regular part of the routine. Now little Johnny or Suzy goes to Mom and says, "Hey, can I have some money for the movies?" Mom hands over $50. The kid goes out and buys 10 bags of heroin. The kid throws a heroin party. And kids die.

At the time of writing this, Nick's girlfriend, Madeline, has been to five treatment centers, and she is living out on the West Side of Chicago—back in active addiction. Andy started working the steps with me, but it didn't last. A short time later, he was back to smoking weed.

I sent him down to Florida to Banyan Treatment Center, where he spent six months in various levels of treatment. I called him Andy the Snail, because it took him so long to make any progress. Eventually, he did great, worked the program, graduated, ran a vape shop, and then kind of fell off the radar.

About three months ago, I got a call from Andy's mom, who was out of town in Florida. "Tim, can you get over to my house in Hinsdale? Andy's cousin called me and said Andy's really messed up. I'm afraid he's doing heroin." I shot over to the house. Andy had overdosed on the sofa. We hit him with Narcan and called the paramedics, who came in and revived him. The paramedics took him out—alive.

I sat there and looked at that sofa. "Son of a bitch. This is the same house and the same sofa my son died on." Andy had been given the second—or third chance—that Nick lost.

Does working with and loving an addict sound like a wasted effort? Well, as hard as it might be to wrap your head around it, just imagine *being* the addict. You begin hating yourself, and you see yourself as deserving of any scorn people have for you. You start believing that you won't be around much longer, so you make even worse, short-sighted choices. You decide to let nature—which usually means death—take its course.

Sometimes addicts enter recovery with the right mindset of the Lord's Prayer: "Give us this day our daily bread" (Matthew 6:11). They enter recovery daily, invest in recovery daily, get on their knees daily, pray for strength to help others daily. But over time, they become less invested in their recovery. Daily becomes every other day. Then weekly. Pretty soon, the lies of addiction come back saying things like, "I've missed you. Why don't we have one more dance before you get serious again?"

And POOF. When that happens, people relapse, and people die.

My recovery is daily. It has to be. In the company of the strong, I am made stronger. I ask God to give me strength and keep me humble. Arrogance is part of addiction. It's hard to become haughty when I start each day on my knees.

CHAPTER 25
PAYING IT FORWARD

All of these stories—Nick's, Abe's, Andy's, mine—show you one thing: Once you get into the game of alcoholism or drug addiction, you have three choices. *You either die, go to prison, or enter recovery.*

Sometimes I try to find the people I served time with. Some of those I thought would do well have ended up back in prison—the majority of them, really. But there are some others who've reached out to me. All of a sudden on Facebook, I'll get a friend request. I accept it without thinking, but I'll get a message, "Hey, Ryan, you are giving me so much."

"God, I surrender. Take away this obsession and compulsion to use, and I swear I'll turn my will and life over to you." I prayed that prayer in prison, and I recommit to it daily.

I look at my old mug shot, and I see a ghost, an empty shell. I remember the bile spilling out of my mouth and crap filling my pants, as I rotted in my dank cell. I wish more songs and movies shared those truths about drugs and alcohol instead of glorifying the highs or downplaying those depths of hell. When I recall those parts of my past, I don't get nostalgic. I get sick. I wouldn't go back to that life for absolutely anything.

That doesn't mean I haven't struggled on the outside. I hurt deeply with each loss. I want to crawl out of my skin when my efforts to help are seen as self-serving—or I'm criticized harshly and publicly for my viewpoints. Instead of reaching for a bag of heroin, I have rules for myself: I go to a meeting or call my sponsor. I work the steps. I reach out to others who are struggling, and I try to flip misery over to its soft underbelly of hope.

I'm not immune from relapse. Any addict who says he is only needs to look at Abe. Abe rolled the dice once more and lost. He's by no means the only person I've lost who was immersed in recovery and sobriety. Heroin keeps whispering and wooing back its prisoners. It doesn't hold grudges. It might look meek, but it's powerful enough to crush anyone. It willingly takes lives—even after just one use. *Just cross over the line one more time*, it begs, before closing its jaws around darkness and death.

In the past 24 months, I've been to 100 plus funerals from heroin use. Each one stabs me in the gut. I don't ever get numb to them. I fucking hate them.

At the same time, around 700 of the addicts I've helped get into recovery are sober today. God has kept me alive to deal hope to those who are trapped by addiction. If I weren't doing that, I'd be joining them. I have to keep soldiering on like my life depends on it, because it does.

On September 19, 2015, I turned 46. The same day, another flame went out. Alana Bianca Carbonara died at age 18 of a heroin overdose in Naperville, Illinois. She video-chatted with a friend just hours before her death. The drugs were making it hard for her to keep her eyes open. Her friend invited her over, where she continued using drugs.

Alana ran in some of the same circles as the kids who would later join my recovery group and Banyan office. She was stunningly beautiful—a blonde haired, blue eyed, high school cheerleader, straight A student—with a sharp wit. She was the life of the party, and she never wanted to disappoint anyone.

Two days later, I got a call from her dad, Scott. After talking with Scott for a few minutes, he said, "Tim, I know you." I never forget a face, but I couldn't see Scott over the phone, so I wasn't sure who he was. "I was in a meeting with you the day your son Nick died." *That Scott.* Scott was the friend I mentioned earlier who'd taken a leak on his neighbor's porch—twice. Scott was in recovery with me. He, too, was my brother.

"My wife and I were in upstate New York for work, when we got the call that Alana had died," Scott told me on the phone that night. "My first thought was that I was going to find out who did this and make them pay. My second thought was, *I need a drink.*"

I understood those feelings only too well.

"But God had other plans," Scott told me. He told me that he did buy a drink while waiting for his flight back to Chicago to comfort his son and make arrangements for Alana. As he swirled the scotch around the glass, watching the glazed ice cubes dissipate into his poison, he debated with the devil: *I could give in, and end up right back in my own addiction. What would it matter, anyway?* He brought it to his nose. The smell of the liquor turned his stomach just enough to make him realize: "*I knew that if I took that drink, there would be two dead. Maybe not today. Not tomorrow. But I would drink myself to death. And that would not honor my daughter.* I pushed it away," Scott told me.

He then told me how his anger and desire for revenge melted during the flight, as he again turned his life and will over to God, even in this time of loss. By the time he landed in Chicago, Scott knew that he would go to any length to use Alana's death to prevent more tragedies.

The next morning, Scott stepped into the West Suburban Fellowship Club, wearing a face of shock. He hadn't slept. He brought his wife, Jocelyn, to talk to me. While he knew Alana struggled with substance abuse, and he'd supported her in and out of several recovery programs, he had no idea that she was using heroin. We talked. I introduced them to Kyle, an addict who had started with heroin accidentally when his friends gave it to him, disguised as ketamine. Kyle had known Alana.

"I'll be at the funeral," I told Scott, offering what I could. "And we'll start a scholarship fund in her honor."

"Does it help at all when these kids see their friends dying? Does it convince any of them to get help?" Jocelyn asked Kyle, searching for some hope in this dark hour.

"It's why I entered treatment," said Kyle, straight faced. "I've seen 8 of my friends die in the past 10 months."

"What can we do to help?" Scott asked.

"Start by telling Alana's story," I said. They were desperate for anything to do. I knew the feeling: when the world around you is spinning, you want to keep moving so you don't fall off.

We exchanged cards, and I introduced them to Denise Crosby from *The Sun-Times*. She interviewed Scott and asked him if she could attend Alana's funeral. She did, along with several hundred of Alana's friends, community and family members, and officers.

Denise sat next to me, as people started milling into the service. "Are these kids okay?" Denise asked me, nodding her head towards a group of kids who seemed out of it.

"Those kids are stoned out of their minds," I told her, as I looked around and saw behaviors familiar to my addiction.

I worked within the active addiction community. I'd heard on the street some of the events surrounding Alana's death, and I knew many of the people Alana spent time with. "That girl over there," I pointed with my face, "She used heroin with Alana the night she died. That other girl on the end," I nodded in another direction, "She hooked Alana up with the person who sold her the heroin that killed her. I know what they must be feeling right now," I said, thinking of my own losses.

When Scott got up to speak, he placed some notes on the podium and grabbed both sides of the lectern—just a few feet from his precious daughter's cold body. Taking a deep breath, he told stories about Alana that made those in attendance laugh and cry. Then Scott changed directions to tell a part of Alana's story that not everyone knew:

Some of you remember the "life of the party" Alana—the wild, free spirited, crazy Alana who said and did things you almost wished you could say and do yourself. So many of the pictures she posted on her well-crafted social media accounts show a happy, living-large Alana, who had the world at her command. What is the face of addiction? It's often the life of the party, the most exciting person in the room. That is one face of addiction.

But there's another face of addiction. How many of you saw her weeping for how unmanageable her life had become? I did. Her mother did. How many of you knew what she did after the party? She went home—alone, terrified, and full of shame. That's another face of addiction.

Look at my Alana now. That is another face of addiction—the cold, lifeless face where many addicts, like Alana, end up way before their time.

But there is another face of addiction: it's my face, the face of someone who struggled but found redemption in active recovery.

Addiction ends in one of two ways: death or recovery. The addiction wants to take your life, like it took the life of my daughter. Recovery wants to redeem your life, giving you unlimited opportunities to live, fight back, and create a life of hope, forgiveness, and strength…

….If you were one of Alana's friends, you are welcome here. If you partied with Alana and enjoyed her as "the life of the party," you are welcome here. If you introduced Alana to heroin, or if you drove her to buy heroin, or you used heroin with Alana, you most certainly are welcome here. And I'd like to talk with you.

And I'd like you to know that I love you. And I'd like you to know that Alana loved you. And if you knew Alana at all, you knew that she would have laid down her life for you.

It's too late for Alana, but it's not too late for you.

If you are on the road to addiction—if you are no longer in the driver's seat of your life—and you get help, Alana's death will have meaning. If you're here in the throes of addiction, don't leave here without talking to me, or Tim with A Man In Recovery Foundation. Tim Ryan understands addiction. He is a recovering addict, and he helps addicts today after he lost his own son to heroin. Kyle is with him. Can you two stand up? Kyle is Alana's age, and he's been in recovery for 10 months. Since that time, this is the 8th funeral he's attended for friends like Alana who died because of their addictions…Please don't leave here without knowing that there is help for you, there is love for you, and there is community for you.

Don't listen to the sweet lies of addiction that tell you that it's too late for you turn back. It isn't. As long as there is life, there is hope. Tonight you can find a loving community of support to help you on your way to recovery and to life, the life that you know you can live, the life Alana would want you to live.

You don't have to live like Alana—terrified, defeated, and alone. And you don't have to die like Alana, either. Please make Alana's death mean something. She would have given everything to be part of your recovery and your healing.

(You can read his full speech here: http://leadershiptherapist. com/2015/10/06/a-story-of-loss-and-hope/)

Several kids who sat in that service talked to me that night and entered recovery within a week. Scott talked with Alana's best friend and helped her get into treatment. I remain very close with Scott and Jocelyn. In fact, they helped me write this book, because they want to help my foundation and mission. They don't want anyone else to experience a loss like theirs or mine.

CHAPTER 26

GRACE ABOUNDS: A SPECIAL ACKNOWLEDGMENT

Going to prison and losing everything brought an unforgettable pain that screamed beyond the cold walls. That's where I finally took the cotton out of my ears and put it in my mouth; I shut up and started listening.

When I listened, I heard this epiphany as if it were shouted in my ear: *Tim, change starts with changing your core beliefs.* Instead of feeling entitled to another drink or high, I had to ask, "How can I be of better service to others?" I had to turn things around and look at them from a perspective that didn't involve manipulating my environment to meet my needs. I had to stop going through the motions just to get someone off my back. I had to start actually embracing the painful process of change. I had to develop faith that grace would carry me to a place I'd never known—but craved.

Before prison, I thought *attending* meetings was recovery. Shit, meetings are just a part of the recovery process. I needed to *live* recovery. I needed to be a better person and constantly work on my character and its defects. I needed to quit letting resentments live in my head, pray for my enemies, and help other people.

I developed a mission *to give back what was so freely given to me.*

So many people want to knock 12-step programs. I believe most of them aren't educated about what the programs do, have never been to one, or don't know what it's like to be completely hopeless, sticking a needle in your arm, drinking a gallon of vodka a day, and wanting to die. Having this simple hope given to me, saying, "If you take this and listen, your life will get better," was a gift of grace. It was an alternative of life that wouldn't erase every loss, but it would bring redemption if I kept moving towards it.

I used to obsess about drinking and doing drugs all the time. That has been lifted by a power greater than myself. I call it God. We've got a great relationship, and I'm not tempting fate anymore. And I'm not tempted to wrestle control out of God's hands anymore, either.

Call it what you want. No, you don't have to believe in God. But you have to have a little faith.

I think of it like this: I've done around 500 skydives. When I jump out of a plane, I have faith that when I throw my parachute, it will open. If it malfunctions, I have faith that when I cut away my reserve, it will open. I don't worry, "I'm going to die." Most of the things I worry about never come true. Grace has carried me.

I've been on the edge of death many times. I've been in the middle of destruction even more. If I recognize the grace in my life, I have to believe that there is definitely something out there distributing it—100 percent, all day long. When I accept it, I can surrender. When I surrender, I'm met with joy and bounty.

On the flip side, shame makes me want to try to control my own life in all the wrong ways. An addict's shame is always driven by fear—fear of people, fear of disapproval, fear of economic situations, fear of what people think, fear of getting sober…the list is endless.

The biggest obstacle I hear from people wanting to turn their lives around is, "I'm not gonna have any fun." They have a *fear of boredom*. Really? It's more fun going out and stealing from your parents, pawning your dad's beautiful whatever, lying, hiding in a parking lot in a shady area to meet a drug dealer, getting high in your car while trying not to get arrested—and doing it all over again the next day?

People don't understand this gift I have and how blessed sobriety is. You know what? I don't need to alter my mind to feel joy. Today, I'm so happy to get out of bed. I can walk and get a cup of coffee. I can go to the bathroom without having to put up a sheet to cover my ass from a cellmate. I can take a long, hot shower—or even a nice cold bath. I can put my feet in grass and not be told, "Put on your shoes. Get back to your cell." I don't take anything for granted today. It's twisted, but going to prison absolutely saved my life—because it gave me my life back.

An addiction might start out with a moment of fun, but it ends with death and destruction. Recovery isn't painless, but it points your feet towards joy—not fear.

I've come a long way. But it never occurs to me to think, "Man, Tim. Look at you! You've got your shit together!" Come on. I'm one drink or drug away from losing everything again. When I ran my life, I made a mess, becoming a human tornado that destroyed anyone and anything in my path.

At the grocery store the other day, a girl yelled, "Oh my God. It's you!" This girl turned to her mom and said, "This is Tim Ryan. He was on the Steve Harvey show. I follow him on Facebook. He's a celebrity."

What a crock of crap, I almost said.

"No, I'm just a drug addict in recovery," I said instead. The mom told me that her son hung himself three years earlier while trying to detox from heroin. This dear woman told me, "I wish you would have been here three years ago to work with my son. Maybe he'd still be alive today."

People don't realize that my mission of dealing hope to the hopeless is 24/7 for me. I'll help a guy who's ready to die and kill himself. I need to go meet with that person. I put myself through this every day, and believe me, it's not easy. I've accepted where God has chosen for me to walk, and I'm going to walk it. I'm one of his warriors, trying to make a difference—and I know we are doing just that. God has provided me with a way to give back, to make ongoing amends, and to pay it forward.

Each month, I speak at around six school assemblies across the country. I've also been the keynote speaker for hospitals and healthcare systems as well as at conferences with court and police officers. In fact, I often hit the road doing a lecture series called, "The Cop, the Convict, and the Kid." Of course, I'm the criminal. Kyle, my young brother in recovery, is the kid. The cop is my friend Richard Wistocki, who is the Detective of Computer Crimes for the Naperville Police Department. Richard talks to parents about how to use technology to know what their kids are doing as a way of keeping them safe. When I went to prison the first time, I told myself that I would never return. I was wrong. I did return. My addiction put me back inside.

When I went to prison the second time, I told myself that I would never return. I was wrong. I did return. But the next time, it was my *recovery* instead of my addiction that put me back inside those prison walls. In the summer of 2016, I got to do something utterly surreal. I went back to Sheridan—speaking about the truth of recovery to all 2,000-plus inmates. Usually, you have to be out of prison for seven years before they will allow you back through the gates to speak. I was welcomed back because of my active work in leading others to recovery; and I got to go back to speak a dozen more times that summer.

Walking back into that place that broke me—but this time as a hope dealer instead of a prisoner—was overwhelming at first. I ran into a guy named Sanchez from Joliet. It was his sixth time in the joint. He had been instrumental in helping me, but there he was back in prison. I ran into probably 10 guys who'd been released and already were back in prison. Each time I walked out of the gates, tremendous humility flooded me. I was no better than these guys, but I'd continued to walk daily in recovery. Within the next few months, I got more than 100 letters from inmates, many of them wanting help to get into sober homes.

My life today isn't perfect. But recovery doesn't suck. God allows me to deal hope with more conviction than any drug dealer I know. I run support groups, advocate for heroin awareness within government, engage in media interviews, and place people in recovery. I was an invited guest at the 2016 State of the Union Address representing awareness of the growing heroin epidemic —a problem that President Obama mentioned within the first few minutes of his speech that night. I've been on major talk shows with Dr. Drew and Steve Harvey. I just spoke to the producers of another major talk show about making an appearance to discuss the heroin epidemic attacking our young people. I've been featured in *Newsweek*. I'm in regular conversations with congressmen and governors. I even met with the U.S. Surgeon General. I couldn't care less about the attention, but if my efforts help drop the stigma of addiction while offering hope, I'm there.

Because of my connections in the addiction community, I can help place people where they can receive treatment. My team members and I currently place 300-plus people a month into treatment. Many of these addicts have no insurance or state insurance. We know where to guide and direct them. We pick them up, get them to detox, and transport them to treatment. We've started programs with police stations so that heroin addicts can walk in; turn in their drugs; say, "I want help;" and get into treatment within four hours.

I've heard some people say, "Stop throwing money at addicts. They are hopeless cases!" They say that until it's their child. Heroin doesn't discriminate. I work with a chief of police, a congressman, a therapist, lawyers, school teachers—all of whom have children addicted to heroin. The youngest heroin addict I've worked with in the past two years is 12 years old; the oldest is 78. They come from all walks of life, race, creed, color, and financial status.

When I lived as an addict, I was just like any addict. I told myself that I had the world by the short hairs. I wanted to believe I was on top of the universe. Nothing could be further from the truth. The more I listened to the lie of addiction tell me how great I was, the more I lost control. Today, I don't listen to lies. I don't tolerate them from myself or anyone else.

Because of where I've been, I've exchanged the lies for raw truth: people fucking die from this. I'm in your face, I'm raw, and I'm real. I'm sick of burying people, and damn it, the hopeless can be hopeful and turn their lives around. We've got to live recovery in every aspect of our lives—every aspect—if we want to recover.

I don't pretend to have all of the answers about recovery, but I know my own story. And I know hundreds if not thousands of people who have cleaned up their lives by working 12-step programs. I could help sober someone up on Lower Wacker Drive in Chicago with the seminal 12-step book written by Bill W. that is still used in Alcoholics Anonymous today, known as "The Big Book," but only if he or she were ready. By ready, I mean open-minded, honest, and willing to go to any lengths to get clean. It's what Tony Robbins and many others meant in saying, "Change happens when the pain of staying the same is greater than the pain of change."

The real work of recovery happens after detox and treatment. Are you willing to put your recovery before everything? Are you willing to purge the diseased thoughts from your mind and patterns of behavior from your life? I have to put my recovery before Shannon, my kids, Kirsten, McKenzie, my job, and my life's work. Because without my recovery, I'm dead in the water and susceptible to falling back into my old patterns of thinking and acting.

Change doesn't happen overnight. It's hard work. That fear will rise up, and you'd better be ready to deal with it. You're going to cry, get mad, and want to use to relieve your pain. Take it minute by minute, hour by hour, and slowly but surely it will get better. My 12-step program comes with something called The Promises.

1. If we are painstaking about this phase of our development, we will be amazed before we are half way through.

2. We are going to know a new freedom and a new happiness.

3. We will not regret the past nor wish to shut the door on it.

4. We will comprehend the word serenity and we will know peace.

5. No matter how far down the scale we have gone, we will see how our experience can benefit others.

6. That feeling of uselessness and self-pity will disappear.

7. We will lose interest in selfish things and gain interest in our fellows.

8. Self-seeking will slip away.

9. Our whole attitude and outlook upon life will change.

10. Fear of people and of economic insecurity will leave us.

11. We will intuitively know how to handle situations which used to baffle us.

12. We will suddenly realize that God is doing for us what we could not do for ourselves.

(*The Big Book*, Bill W., Alcoholics Anonymous, pp. 83-84)

These promises are specific and bold in what they deliver. And what does it take? Recovery. In the last few years, every one of those promises have come true tenfold in my life. And I want of that inner peace and happiness—so I keep digging deeper.

That's why I'm a man in recovery. I will always be *in recovery*. Even as I'm guiding others into getting help, I can't ever take my own recovery for granted. I still work with a sponsor, I still go to four meetings a week, and I still sponsor people. I get out of myself, and as a friend says, I "chop wood and carry water."

Some people can go to church on Sunday, spend their hour, and feel good about themselves. I go to church every day in my own mind and head. I use prayer and meditation throughout the day. When I start getting into my self-centeredness, I stop and remember what a friend always said to me: "What have you done to get out of yourself and help someone else today?"

More than once, I've found myself slipping, and I have to slow down and stop trying to do so much. I need family balance. I need my kid time. I need them in my life. The other day, I took Max, Abby, McKenzie, and Kirsten to Portillo's to eat. We laughed and had a blast together. I need that kind of joy, the simple things in life, to keep me balanced.

I never wanted to be a crusader. I wanted to be a professional water-skier. But I am a grateful recovering alcoholic and drug addict—thankful that God kept politely asking to help me get healthy until I slammed myself against a wall. I'm thrilled that He lets me make amends for my shame. And he allows me to show love and offer help to others like Andy, Abe, Scott, and hundreds more who have been turned inside out by addiction.

All that "good" stuff that I've done so far in the four years since I've been in recovery? It wasn't me. It was God using me, as long as I stayed committed to daily recovery.

My life is like a pile of old newspapers. If I peel them back far enough to get beyond the yellowing sections, I see white, unblemished parts—like bright-eyed, innocent Maggie. I think about her sometimes, because I'm sure she didn't waste years of her life chasing demons. She found God early, and she stayed with Him. She had nothing to recover from. If I could see Maggie today, I'd say, "I'm sorry. I was just a young kid lost in addiction." Then I'd thank her for being a light in my dark world, for showing me a God I wouldn't submit to for many more years. And I'd give her a big hug. (I guarantee she's still cute as a button.)

Michelle McCormick and Haley Dean were right more than 30 years ago when they had the courage to speak the truth with love: "Tim, you're gonna die. You need help. You're just out of control with this." *Thank you for having the courage and the concern to speak up, even when I wasn't ready to hear your words.* It took me

30 years, but I'm ready. And I use similar words when I plead with other addicts today.

Mom and Dad have loved me unconditionally since they first became my parents. And they wanted to use "tough-love" with me. *Thank you for loving me and not giving up on me.* Today I know how hard it is to practice tough love. But that's what I try to offer others. Addicts and their family members need to hear the straight-up truth about what an addiction will do. But they also need love—the kind of love that only one who has walked 30 years in those broken-down, going-nowhere shoes can offer with sincerity.

Shannon, Max, Tanner, and Abby have walked with me through the darkest periods of my life. To them, I hope to impart the message: *I know that because of me, you went through darkness and hell that you did not deserve. I find myself awed and humbled that you still stand with me, in spite of all the ways that I let you down. When I get out of bed each day, I give God thanks for you. And I ask that He will give you an extra measure of grace to make up for the example I failed to show you when I was in the depths of my own despair.*

Nick, you are with me every day. I know you are looking down on me and helping to guide my steps. I miss you. I wish that we had had a chance to speak across the country and share our story. I am carrying on with your wishes. You fuel me.

From *dope to hope*, I am a man in recovery.

Tim Ryan

P.S. To join me on my crusade, you can learn more or connect at AMIRF.org.

ABOUT THE AUTHOR

By his own account, Tim Ryan shouldn't be here. But as he states, "Where there is life, there is hope."

Known as The Hope Dealer, Tim is a successful entrepreneur, grateful recovering heroin addict and alcoholic, nationally ranked barefoot water skier—and truth-talking, convicted felon.

- As a business leader in a high-tech industry, Tim made and lost millions.

- As a father and husband, Tim paved the way for his own son's demise by deadly drugs.

- As a heroin addict, Tim is a walking miracle. He's overdosed eight times, was pronounced clinically dead three, and suffered two minor heart attacks. He's been arrested more than 10 times and served prison time alongside known gang leaders—many of whom became his closest confidants in recovery.

- As the founder of A Man in Recovery Foundation, author of From Dope to Hope, and motivational speaker, Tim's mission is to help *one addict at a time* transform their lives from *dope to hope.*

Heroin didn't make Tim a better person. It stole more than half of his life. But since walking out of prison, he's paid back every waking minute—dealing hope to addicts and their loved ones.

Tim works closely with law enforcement and legislators to address the addiction epidemic at its core. He's helped raise awareness, teach relapse prevention techniques, host forums, encourage treatment, and institute programs to help addicts end up in recovery instead of prison. He's passionate about placing any willing addict with a need, regardless of insurance, into a recovery program.

In recognition for his work, Tim has been a featured thought leader in numerous national media—including *USA Today*, *Newsweek*, "The Steve Harvey Show with Dr. Drew," and dozens of nationally syndicated radio shows. He was an invited guest by the U.S. President to the 2016 State of the Union Address.

Tim has the unique gift to break through with brutal honesty and compassion to anyone who has lost the will to live, because he was once there himself—on the edge of losing his own life to addiction. His story is real, his style is raw, and his ability to ignite hope in others is unprecedented.

Visit www.AMIRF.org to learn more about Tim's work, order bulk copies of his book, or schedule him to speak.